THE POETRY BUSINESS SCHOOL

LUSH

HarperCollins*Publishers*

THE POETRY BUSINESS SCHOOL

Deborah Alma
Mark Constantine OBE
with Kate Downey-Evans CPsychol

HarperCollins*Publishers*
1 London Bridge Street
London SE1 9GF
WilliamCollinsBooks.com

HarperCollins*Publishers*
Macken House
39/40 Mayor Street Upper
Dublin 1
D01 C9W8
Ireland

First published by Cosmetic Warriors Ltd and HarperCollins*Publishers* 2025

A catalogue record for this book is available from the British Library

Library of Congress Cataloging-in-Publication Data has been applied for

ISBN 978-0-00-875764-9

PLU 219452

Written by Mark Constantine, Deborah Alma and Kate Downey-Evans
Foreword by Holly Tucker
Cover illustration: Kate Ellistone
Art direction: Suzie Hackney
Artworking: Lily Thomas and Julia Lawrence
Project editor for LUSH: Matt Fairhall
Project editor for HarperCollins*Publishers*: Caitlin Doyle
Proofreader: Helena Caldon
Production controller: Sarah Burke

Printed and bound by GPS Group, Bosnia-Herzegovina

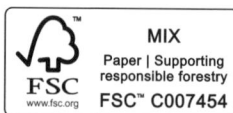

'Get me poets as managers. Poets are our original systems thinkers. They look at our most complex environments and they reduce the complexity to something they begin to understand.'

Sidney Harman
Founder of Harman Industries

'... poetry has defined business mainly by excluding it. Business does not exist in the world of poetry, and therefore by implication it has become everything that poetry is not – a world without imagination, enlightenment, or perception.'

Extract from *Business and Poetry* by Dana Gioia, taken from *Can Poetry Matter? Essays on Poetry and American Culture*, 1983

For Maya Rowland and Pat Edwards. For their friendship and unswerving belief that a Poetry Pharmacy was a good idea.
Deborah Alma

For my grandson, Dexter.
Mark Constantine

EST. 2019

POETRY

PHARMACY

WITH

LUSH

Contents

Page:	
12	Foreword by Holly Tucker MBE
14	Preface by Mark Constantine OBE: It Hasn't Come To That Yet
18	Dragon's Den With A Heart
32	Chapter One Business as a Poem – On listening to your body, the value of intuition, the strength in being vulnerable and of living with uncertainty
48	Chapter Two Business as a Nightclub – On avoiding burnout, coping with pressure and achieving perspective
62	Chapter Three Business as Creativity – On overcoming fear of finance, and looking to the future
74	Chapter Four Business as Neighbourhood – On working with people, and leadership
88	Chapter Five Business as a Garden – On growth, scaling-up and ruthless prioritising
108	Chapter Six Business as a Journey – On taking risks and authenticity
130	Acknowledgements
131	Illustration and Photography Credits
133	Poem Acknowledgements
135	Index of Poems, Poets and First Lines
138	Quoted Material Acknowledgements
140–141	Author Biographies

Poetry Pharmacy
36 High St, Bishop's Castle, Shropshire SY9 5BQ
www.poetrypharmacy.co.uk

Lush Spa Oxford Street
175–179 Oxford St, London W1D 2JS
www.lush.com

Foreword
By Holly Tucker MBE

Over the past few years, we've all been through the wringer somewhat, haven't we? The world has been a relentless teacher (to put it politely!), throwing curveballs at every turn. The pandemic turned our lives upside down, forcing us to scramble for new ways to live, work and – let's face it – simply breathe. Add to that the seismic shifts in our business landscapes, especially here in the UK, where the cutting of ties with Europe has felt like the rug being pulled out from under our feet. It's been a lot to take in.

So, when I first heard about this book, I was rather intrigued. A book that marries poetry with business? I'm sure a few of you are wondering, 'What on earth do those two worlds have in common?' One is often seen as being soft and whimsical, a world of emotion, creativity and imagination. The other, hard-nosed and practical, driven by numbers, strategies and bottom lines. But let me tell you, this book is about to flip that thinking rather entirely on its head.

Having spent more than twenty years in the small business world through founding Holly & Co and, before that, Notonthehighstreet, I've been on my own journey of understanding the connection between business and creativity – and the immense power of their combination.

We often look at Mr. Business as being the anchor, the pillar of certainty, the one who's always right (not Mark! He's one of the few exceptions). But so often, it's Mrs. Creativity who makes business happen. She gives permission for the never-thought-of-befores, stokes the mind to believe in 'what-ifs' and ultimately fuels the best businesses to shine. It's not just about working together but working in unity.

Deb and Mark are two souls who've not only embraced the intersection of these worlds but have thrived there. They have come together in a way that is nothing short of magical. Through their dialogue, through their shared wisdom and vulnerability, they've created something truly special here.

As I read through their words, I couldn't help but feel a deep connection to the challenges they've faced – challenges that echo what so many of us have been grappling with along the way. The constant juggling act between keeping our businesses afloat and staying true to our creative and emotional selves. The exhaustion that comes with endless decision-making and the burnout that sneaks up on us when we least expect it. They don't shy away from these realities; instead, they lean into them, finding strength and solace in poetry.

What makes this book so powerful is that it isn't just a guide for business growth or a manual for success (though you'll undoubtedly find plenty of practical advice and inspiration here). It's a gentle reminder that at its core, business is a deeply human endeavour. It's about people, ideas and emotions. It's about connection, creativity and having the courage to see the world differently. And in the face of the challenges we now face as a society – with our communities and planet under such immense strain – this synergy between business and creativity is becoming more than just a philosophy. It's evolving into a mandate for founders and business leaders to use their incredible strength for more than just the bottom line; to use it to do something good.

And that's where poetry comes in. Poetry, with its ability to distil the essence of our experiences into a few carefully chosen words, helps us tap into that deeper well of understanding. It invites us to pause, reflect and see the familiar in a whole new light. In a world that's constantly pushing us to go faster and to do more, poetry gives us permission to slow down and just be present. It's a way of connecting with ourselves and others, finding meaning in the mundane somehow, and beauty in the chaos.

For those of you who might feel stuck in your business right now, this book is a breath of fresh air. It offers a new perspective and shows you that business doesn't have to be all about the grind or the numbers (and Lord knows it feels like that sometimes, doesn't it?!). It's a great reminder that business is often a creative act, a form of expression and a way to communicate your ideas with the world.

Deb and Mark's journey together is an invitation to explore your own path and find your balance between the demands of your business and the needs of your soul. It's a call to embrace the unexpected, find joy in the small things and remember that, at the end of the day, we are all in this together. So, even though this might seem like a strange combination – to bring poetry into the world of business – it could profoundly shift you into fresh thinking. Language has the power to make us question what we know to be true. And I can't wait to see how this book helps us all to think the unthinkable – in the best possible way.

I hope you find it as inspiring, uplifting and comforting as I have.

Holly Tucker MBE
Founder of Holly & Co
Founder of Notonthehighstreet
UK Ambassador to Creative Small Businesses

POETRY
PHARMACY

Insomnia

Handmade at 76 High Street, Bishop's Castle

There is a magic made by melody:
Heart, that sinks through failing
To the subaqueous stillness of the
Held in the arms of rhythm and

Preface: It Hasn't Come To That Yet

Mark Constantine OBE
Lush Co-founder & CEO

It hasn't come to that yet.

I have a favourite badge with 'It hasn't come to that yet' written on it. Recently it did come to that – my seven-year-old grandson died of cancer. When life events like that come along, I find solace in poetry.

That doesn't work for everyone. Famously, I read a poem early every morning to Mo, my wife and fellow inventor, until she eventually told me, 'I'm not really into poetry.' My friend and fellow entrepreneur Holly Tucker runs The Independent Awards scheme and I (with a little help from my Lush managers) had been one of the judges. We loved the Poetry Pharmacy in Bishop's Castle, Shropshire the most and wanted it to win. It made it to the finals. Deb Alma, the owner, on hearing about the loss of my seven-year-old grandson, made me a Poetry Pharmacy prescription: *'For Days when the World is too much with us. Distillations, panaceas, restoratives & cures especially prescribed for Mark Constantine (not to be swallowed except metaphorically).'* These tiny pieces of poetry are life-savers.

When I found my father, who was lost to me for so many years, he then died shortly after and I realised that had I not known him, I would have been denied the common human connection of knowing your father upon his death. Those that haven't known their dad will understand. It's what binds us all.

So, when you see Wordsworth's poetry on Lush's bags and in our shop windows, you will know that at Lush, we want to be there for you 'when the world is too much with us.' We may not always be able to hit the spot, but we will be trying.

PS
What I didn't say was that the prescription came with a gift, *Poems That Make Grown Men Cry*, edited by Anthony and Ben Holden, and that I chose a lullaby from within this anthology to slip into my pocket on the day of the funeral – Dexter's coffin was transported in a carriage pulled by four black horses.

All the Pretty Horses

Hush-by, Don't you cry
Go to sleep a little baby
When you wake you shall find
All the pretty little horses

Blacks and bays, dapples and greys
Coach and six a little horses
When you wake you shall find
All the pretty little horses

Hush-by, Don't you cry
Go to sleep a little baby
When you wake you shall find
All the pretty little horses

Anonymous

Dragon's Den With A Heart

Hello there

I was a judge in the recent Holly & Co competition and I wanted you to win. Disappointing.... Now everything is out of stock? Doubly disappointing. If it's not out of stock but a system error and you would like to sell me stuff, drop me a line.

Mark Constantine

Deb

This email from Mark came out of the blue after the Poetry Pharmacy had been on The Independent Awards shortlist for the High Street Shop award in a competition run by entrepreneur and champion of small businesses, Holly Tucker. We had no idea that Lush were judging us and that they'd visited us as secret shoppers earlier in 2021.

**From Deb
To Mark**

Sat, 11 Dec 2021, 5:02pm

Dear Mark,

That's incredibly kind of you! Thank you so much!

This morning we were delighted to have been featured in *The Guardian* gift guide, but as a largely single-handed small business, we have been a little overwhelmed. I hope to be back in stock by the end of the week and will update the website accordingly. But do let me know what you'd like and I'd be happy to send it?

Warmest wishes,
Deborah

*Right: Deb outside the Poetry Pharmacy
in Bishop's Castle, 2024.*

So started a developing friendship with Mark, and then more widely, members of the Lush team, with our tiny business in Tiny Town, Bishop's Castle, Shropshire.

Lush needs no introduction, and the Poetry Pharmacy needs some, which I'll come to later. I started to learn that these two businesses, with their huge differences in scale, have a make-it-up-from-scratch spirit in common, and are underpinned by a belief in something. Both businesses come from personal passions and imaginative ways of doing things. They are both good examples of business as a creative act. Both have original products, new aesthetics and new ways of doing business. I concluded that business, like poetry, may be a vision of the future, something that hasn't happened yet. Business people, like artists, may be more comfortable with risk, and like artists, are concerned with the communication of an idea.

From Mark
To Deb

Sat, 11 Dec 2021, 5:51pm

I really feel Thomas Hardy's poems the most, but I often quote Kipling, especially 'A Pict Song', and pretty much everything from Gibran's 'The Prophet'. I have always wanted to do a poems for business anthology. So from 'A Pict Song' there's a wonderful bit where Kipling likens the mistletoe in the oak to the moth in the cloak, to the rat at the rope. He shows how much they must love what they do. Understanding the natural forces of decay is important if you are to run a business without despair.

Happy for you to choose and feel free to spend a little more if it would make a lovely example of your wares.

There were three of us here at Lush doing my visits and judgings. I'm not sure if the other judges were as enthusiastic (story of my life).

Anyway, we love you.
Mark

This began a dialogue, sometimes by email, sometimes by Zoom or phone calls, and sometimes in person, with me slightly bewildered by Mark's interest in the Poetry Pharmacy. He not only loved it, but seemed to take it more seriously as a grown-up business idea than I did. He saw it as a business that had potential for significant growth, something that hadn't really occurred to me, except in my wildest dreams.

A Pict Song

('The Winged Hats' – Puck of Pook's Hill)

Rome never looks where she treads.
  Always her heavy hooves fall
On our stomachs, our hearts or our heads;
  And Rome never heeds when we bawl.
Her sentries pass on—that is all,
  And we gather behind them in hordes,
And plot to reconquer the Wall,
  With only our tongues for our swords.

We are the Little Folk—we!
  Too little to love or to hate.
Leave us alone and you'll see
  How we can drag down the State!
We are the worm in the wood!
  We are the rot at the root!
We are the taint in the blood!
  We are the thorn in the foot!

Mistletoe killing an oak—
  Rats gnawing cables in two—
Moths making holes in a cloak—
  How they must love what they do!
Yes—and we Little Folk too,
  We are busy as they—
Working our works out of view—
  Watch, and you'll see it some day!

No indeed! We are not strong,
  But we know Peoples that are.
Yes, and we'll guide them along
  To smash and destroy you in War!
We shall be slaves just the same?
  Yes, we have always been slaves,
But you—you will die of the shame,
  And then we shall dance on your graves!

     We are the Little Folk, we, etc.

Rudyard Kipling

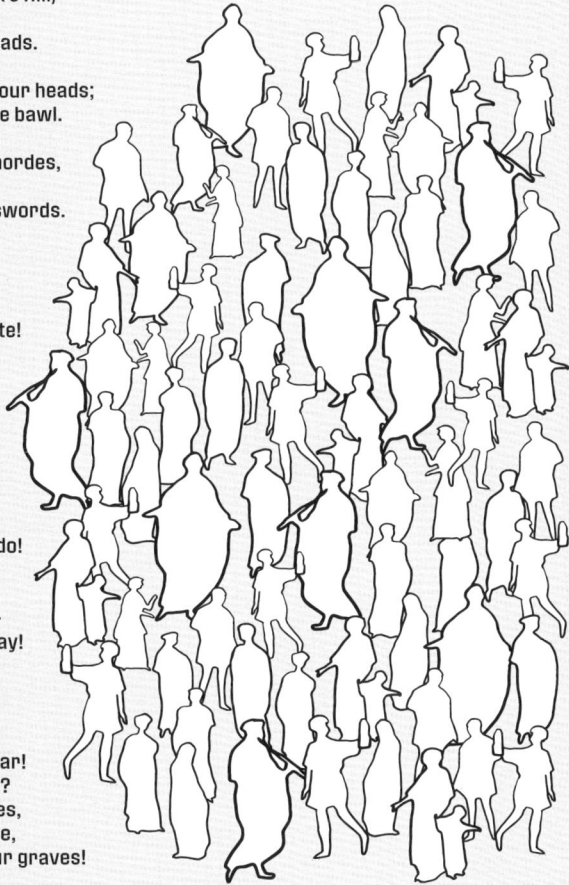

From Mark
To Deb

Sat, 2 Jul 2022, 12:13pm

Dear Deborah,

Business is never-ending and any task is possible, no matter how daunting. You eat an elephant one mouthful at a time. I would add that you can start a business at any age, as experience is a far better teacher than business school.

So, for example, a plan may be:

1. Recruit and train London-based staff, including someone to talk to prospective partners. Remember, Tim Waterstone describes how he did what his staff told him. People who are into poetry are passionate about sharing their knowledge. Find some.
2. Get a London shop in a popular location. Now is a great time to get a good deal. If it's a good-enough spot, you can always get out of it should you need to.
3. Open said shop.
4. Make a few deals and go from there.

Dive deep. There is a resurgence in books and bookshops. Amazon has cleared the way for a concept such as yours. Booksellers know almost nothing about you. Surprise them. Inspire them.

Avoid taking partners or other shareholders. Do it on a shoestring. Pay your way with profit, not investment.

I assume your lifelong aim is to get everyday folk to embrace the power of poetry to change their lives. It may have taken you a lifetime to get there but that shouldn't deter you from making hay now that the sun is shining. Your idea is so unknown.

When Mark kept bringing up 'your London shop, which in your case, you have not got', I laughed – every time, I laughed! It seemed so beyond what I believed myself to be capable of. Wasn't it already too much for me? Wasn't I already exhausted by working in my Poetry Pharmacy in Bishop's Castle, hoovering at the end of the day and cleaning the toilet, as well as all the admin around being a bookseller? Not to mention we make our own products – poems inside pill capsules for various emotional ailments. I was already doing too much. He just didn't seem to understand!

Right: Colour Therapy poetry pills are one example of a range of poetic medicines available over the counter at the Poetry Pharmacy. Small scrolls of poetic solace are printed on banana paper.

POETRY PHARMACY

Colour Therapy

Red

Verditter Blu

From Mark
To Deb

I am not sure what constitutes a poet. Did Henry Reed write much poetry?
I learnt from Clive James' poems that he wanted people 'to get by heart and read aloud'. I suppose it doesn't matter; this will do.

We talked of poetry being ruthless. Not in a horrid way, rather a stripping-down way. If your purpose is to show how life-enhancing poetry can be and you stumble upon a concept so effective at doing this, then everything you do that isn't that ends up working against your purpose.

It can be reassuring to 'name the parts' but if your purpose is to show everyone how beautiful the almond blossom is, then you don't want to be cleaning the toilets, rolling every little poetic tidbit, or cleaning the floor of your lovely London shop, which in your case you have not got.

I don't know that you have to have a shop in every town. One on the King's Road will do. Or perhaps one next door to Daunt's on the Marylebone High Street, and then others will take it from there.

Naming of Parts

To-day we have naming of parts. Yesterday,
We had daily cleaning. And tomorrow morning,
We shall have what to do after firing. But to-day,
To-day we have naming of parts. Japonica
Glistens like coral in all of the neighbouring gardens,
    And today we have naming of parts.

This is the lower sling swivel. And this
Is the upper sling swivel, whose use you will see,
When you are given your slings. And this is the piling swivel,
Which in your case you have not got. The branches
Hold in the gardens their silent, eloquent gestures,
    Which in our case we have not got.

This is the safety-catch, which is always released
With an easy flick of the thumb. And please do not let me
See anyone using his finger. You can do it quite easy
If you have any strength in your thumb. The blossoms
Are fragile and motionless, never letting anyone see
    Any of them using their finger.

And this you can see is the bolt. The purpose of this
Is to open the breech, as you can see. We can slide it
Rapidly backwards and forwards: we call this
Easing the spring. And rapidly backwards and forwards
The early bees are assaulting and fumbling the flowers:
    They call it easing the spring.

They call it easing the Spring: it is perfectly easy
If you have any strength in your thumb: like the bolt,
And the breech, and the cocking-piece and the point of balance,
Which in our case we have not got; and the almond-blossom
Silent in all of the gardens and the bees going backwards and forwards,
    For to-day we have naming of parts.

Henry Reed

Fri, 8 Jul 2022, 2:13pm

'...but if your purpose is to show everyone how beautiful the almond blossom is then you don't want to be; cleaning the toilets, rolling every little poetic tidbit',

Yes, yes – wise. It's something I heard from when we first met, and I have made lots of changes already. It has been hard to step away from my early days where I was working with an old friend and my son to set up lots of our 'systems' and I had adopted a habit of protecting them from 'my' unpleasant jobs. I have since invested in more help and I'm less afraid to say clearly that someone else clearing the cafe tables frees me up to do other work.

I looked at London rents in those places and ran away... I think I am building a space, in a particular place, with its therapy in slowness and hills, and may eye up the building next door here in Bishop's Castle before I venture to the King's Road in London! What was that TV series in the 70s with David Carradine? *Kung Fu?*

Thank you for your sage advice!

Another poem for you? Both stillness after a journey and something ahead...
D

Arrival

Not conscious
    that you have been seeking
      suddenly
    you come upon it

the village in the Welsh hills
    dust free
   with no road out
but the one you came in by.

    A bird chimes
   from a green tree
the hour that is no hour
    you know. The river dawdles
to hold a mirror for you
where you may see yourself
    as you are, a traveller
     with the moon's halo
   above him, whom has arrived
    after long journeying where he
     began, catching this
   one truth by surprise
that there is everything to look forward to.

R. S. Thomas

How flattering for someone in his position with spas and hundreds of shops. How many? 900? All over the world. How flattering that he should think that the Poetry Pharmacy was a good idea. He said it a lot; finally, finally, after a three-hour meeting in Poole in the Spring of 2023, he actually got me to hear him. He meant it. He believed in its potential to expand more than I did. He suggested that he would mentor me to get there. What could I do but say 'Yes. Alright then. Thank you.' It was to be explicitly not a relationship of investment, but of advice and guidance. He said: 'Look back at our conversations. I said it from the start.'

I had believed that we were working together on a poetry anthology for business people. What we have come to instead is this book; a story of a Dragon's Den with a heart, a mentoring relationship from one successful business to another fledgling business. Our dialogue, it turned out, was a mentoring exchange in poetry and a slightly pushy-like-a-parent You Can Do It manual. Some of our conversations overlapped with, and included, the warm and wise Kate Downey-Evans, Mark's business coach and founder of The Green Door Project, with its explicit subtitle, Transforming Business as a Force for Good. Kate is a self-confessed poetry sceptic and some of her down-to-earth advice is also included in these exchanges.

As a bookseller and editor, I think this book you're holding is the oddest I've ever seen, apart from maybe *Zen and the Art of Motorcycle Maintenance* or *How to Avoid Huge Ships*. We're writing it in real-time, almost like a journal of the Poetry Pharmacy's journey to open a second branch, very ambitiously in Central London. This was entirely Mark's idea, and we'll see where it goes now that I've been inspired by his belief and energy, and have adopted his idea too. And maybe, dear Small Business Owner, you might learn as I'm learning.

Although it might seem that the worlds of poetry and business are miles apart, I'm convinced that poetry has a significant role to play in developing a more philosophical engagement with the working practices of the corporate world, and in helping business people in both their thinking and in navigating any uncertainties.

I came to this project with some trepidation. I see myself first of all as a poet and arts practitioner, but of course, the Poetry Pharmacy is a small and emerging successful business. I am a business person. I hadn't quite seen myself in that way before.

Fri, 8 Jul 2022, 9:50pm

Thank you for the package. Lots to love.

I loved the rescue kit, but my favourite was the lovely surprise in the envelope – the 'don't panic' letterpress card. It's often the simplest things that are the most fun.

It has been very busy up to now. I am looking forward to a period of reading and birding. Should you want to listen to birdsong, my Twitter [X] account @markatlush has a bird sound recorded on the same day sometime in the last two decades by friends or me.

I have been awake quite a bit at night recently and now have my Poetry Pharmacy Insomnia tablets close at hand. Tonight it was Colette – very profound:

'In its early stages, insomnia is almost an oasis in which those who have to think or suffer darkly take refuge.'

1

Business as a Poem

On listening to your body, the value of intuition, the strength in being vulnerable and of living with uncertainty

I mean Negative Capability, that is when man is capable of being in uncertainties, mysteries, doubts, without any irritable reaching after fact and reason.

John Keats

Deb

A poem at its best can be a nuanced dance between the intellect and the emotions, and often at its heart lies a profound connection to intuition, and to uncharted landscapes. Emotions often manifest physically – the quickened heartbeat, the knot in the stomach, or a tingling sensation on the skin. Poets transform these sensations into metaphors. The rhythms of the words echo these heartbeats and embrace the deeply felt to shape the work, moving beyond logic into new territory.

From Mark To Deb

The first lesson of business is that it is a way of making money while pleasing yourself. I don't remember when I realised that business is never done – I'm not sure, despite always being in business. I recommend the point of view that this is an aim unto itself.

It's no longer cool to be a playboy, but Eugen Boissevain was described by his friend Alyse Powers as 'handsome, reckless, mettlesome as a stallion breathing the first morning air, he would laugh at himself, indeed laugh at everything, with a laugh that scattered melancholy as the wind scatters the petals of the fading poppy... He had the gift of the aristocrat and could adapt himself to all circumstances... his blood was testy, adventurous, quixotic, and he faced life as an eagle faces its flight.'

And we can add that he was a businessman who, along with his two brothers, set up Boissevain & Co. and made his fortune by importing coffee beans from Java between 1917 and 1928. The markup was huge and Eugen said he couldn't believe how much people would pay for the lowly coffee bean. While they started in Amsterdam taking advantage of the Dutch colonies in Indonesia, they ended up in New York. In his apartment block Eugen had the well-known writer and socialist Max Eastman and Charlie Chaplin as tenants.

Edna St. Vincent Millay was a bi-sexual poet, feminist and political activist who won the 1923 Pulitzer Prize for her poem 'The Ballad of the Harp Weaver'. She met Eugen while playing charades at a party. They married and had an open relationship.

So there you have it — two people who wished to please themselves and who could as easily be living in New York today, who lived the life they wanted, funded by the coffee money.

What If This Road

What if this road, that has held no surprises
these many years, decided not to go
home after all; what if it could turn
left or right with no more ado
than a kite-tail? What if its tarry skin
were like a long, supple bolt of cloth,
that is shaken and rolled out, and takes
a new shape from the contours beneath?
And if it chose to lay itself down
in a new way; around a blind corner,
across hills you must climb without knowing
what's on the other side; who would not hanker
to be going, at all risks? Who wants to know
a story's end, or where a road will go?

Sheenagh Pugh

I have always said that no one can suggest a business for another person and now here I am doing just that. With Kate as my business coach, I have really felt taught. I could pretend that I had forgotten the lessons that running businesses for forty years had taught me. However, I have never felt so well guided.

The other day when we discussed business schools, she expressed some cynicism. As you start a business school session, you might know the way it will go, but what if the session chose to lay itself down in a new way? I think there is a desperate need for a new sort of business school. One that teaches real business, that mentors those in the arena and marries good education with high principles and ethics.

'It is not the critic who counts; not the man who points out how the strong man stumbles, or where the doer of deeds could have done them better. The credit belongs to the man who is actually in the arena, whose face is marred by dust and sweat and blood; who strives valiantly; who errs, who comes short again and again, because there is no effort without error and shortcoming; but who does actually strive to do the deeds; who knows great enthusiasms, the great devotions; who spends himself in a worthy cause; who at the best knows in the end the triumph of high achievement, and who at the worst, if he fails, at least fails while daring greatly, so that his place shall never be with those cold and timid souls who neither know victory nor defeat.' Theodore Roosevelt

Many folk need to go to business school to learn about the bits of business that they don't know about. But what if they learnt how to build a business without a bank? What if they learnt to grow it without venture capital and without going public, and adopted the principles of a co-op or staff-owned company? What if the school continued on into the lifetime of its student providing guidance? Imagine a world where businesses held principles like the Quaker companies of old. I would send everyone to Kate's school.

Mark

I think I'm starting to understand what we're attempting here, and I think it needs a bit more business soul-searching from me than I had anticipated, which is both exciting and a challenge!

To get it going, then, I have looked through some poems that appeal to me at the moment and did it that way round. I wondered what it was that I was seeking in terms of advice or support from a poetry-speaking business mentor.

There were a few poems I liked, and it was hard to pin it to one, but I've chosen 'The Road Not Taken' by Robert Frost (it can be a real cliché of a poem, but a great one nonetheless).

I have described the Poetry Pharmacy, and its development, as exploring to the ends of the fingers of a glove. Actually now (and I am very conscious of all the things I get offered or asked to do now and have to turn down) it is more like 'The Road Not Taken'. There are other roads that look tantalising and that are not explored. And that the paths I choose for the business and myself become necessarily the 'right' one?

The Road Not Taken

Two roads diverged in a yellow wood,
And sorry I could not travel both
And be one traveler, long I stood
And looked down one as far as I could
To where it bent in the undergrowth;

Then took the other, as just as fair,
And having perhaps the better claim,
Because it was grassy and wanted wear;
Though as for that the passing there
Had worn them really about the same,

And both that morning equally lay
In leaves no step had trodden black.
Oh, I kept the first for another day!
Yet knowing how way leads on to way,
I doubted if I should ever come back.

I shall be telling this with a sigh
Somewhere ages and ages hence:
Two roads diverged in a wood, and I—
I took the one less traveled by,
And that has made all the difference.

Robert Frost

From Deb
To Mark

Something a friend said to me about the business has stuck in my head for some reason. It's the thing I've battled with all my life actually, in one way or another, and for the first time felt myself accepting it. That's not like me.

It was connected to me chatting about the future of the Poetry Pharmacy and where it might go in terms of any commercial success, and she said something about me maybe being too old for the next steps.

I did my degree in my forties and bought a vintage ambulance. I did an MA in my fifties and then some teaching. I started this business three years ago. I've never believed in this too-late-now attitude, but I now have white hair and a bad back and I am starting to think maybe she's right?!

I found this, 'Table' by Edip Cansever, to counteract that...

D

Table

A man filled with the gladness of living
Put his keys on the table,
Put flowers in a copper bowl there.
He put his eggs and milk on the table.
He put there the light that came in through the window,
Sounds of a bicycle, sound of a spinning wheel.
The softness of bread and weather he put there.
On the table the man put
Things that happened in his mind.
What he wanted to do in life,
He put that there.
Those he loved, those he didn't love,
The man put them on the table too.
Three times three make nine:
The man put nine on the table.
He was next to the window next to the sky;
He reached out and placed on the table endlessness.
So many days he had wanted to drink a beer!
He put on the table the pouring of that beer.
He placed there his sleep and his wakefulness;
His hunger and his fullness he placed there.

Now that's what I call a table!
It didn't complain at all about the load.
It wobbled once or twice, then stood firm.
The man kept piling things on.

Edip Cansever
Translated from the Turkish
by Julia Clare Tillinghast & Richard Tillinghast

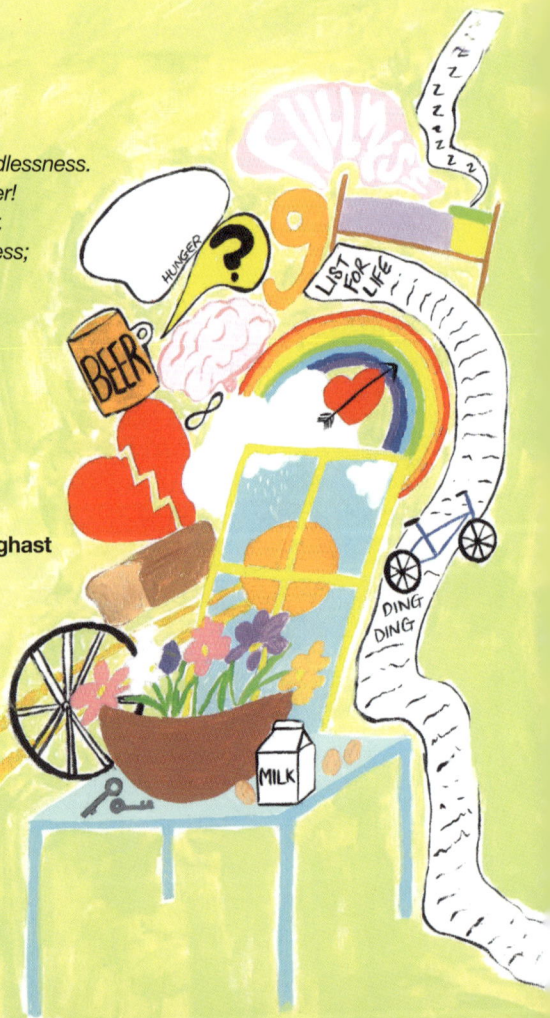

Kayley Thomas started as a part-time sales assistant in Lush Taunton at the age of seventeen, whilst studying Holistics at East Devon College. Two years later, she famously complained to Mark that Lush was taking too long to open its first spa. He told her, 'you do it then', so she helped develop Lush's spa brand, including its first treatments, and supported the opening of spas in Japan, Korea and North America. She is also his PA and, like Kate, a poetry sceptic. As Mark's PA, Kayley was copied in on all of our exchanges and had to endure a lot of poetry.

From Kayley To Deb

I'm surprised at how pertinent this poem is for me. I often think of the array of opportunities that arise for the Lush Spa and how my 'beliefs' shape the next steps. Are they right? Have I enabled something to flourish or unintentionally missed something?

In regards to the age thing, it's very interesting because I've had the complete opposite experience. I've always felt 'too young.' Too young to be making big decisions, too young to address senior meetings.

I love the idea of filling the table with more. I want to look back and think, wow haven't I done a lot! But having the confidence, conviction and self-belief is still something I'm waiting to grow into. I have to have a word with myself and say don't expect at forty to suddenly be fine with leading that big meeting (or whatever it is).

I love these two poems ['The Road Not Taken' and 'Table'] that you sent to Mark. The first one has an unusual angle but I take a few things from it. How time and memories tint our reality and how fear can hold us back. Lean into love. The second reminds me to live in the moment and enjoy all that I have in work and life. Don't consume yourself with worry. Not sure if this is what everyone else takes from them :)

Thanks for sharing, it was more interesting than I imagined (sorry).

I have learnt that we create the businesses that reflect us at the top of our game. We tend to be the reason the business is what it is; a success or failure.

'An Optimistic Paean to False Starts' by Rabindranath Tagore

Life's honouring deeds we start and do not do –
I know, I know that these are counted too.
The flowers that do not come to flower
but drop to earth and lose their power,
the rivers that run dry in desert, never to renew,
I know, I know that these are counted too.
Today's intentions that are not seen through,
I know, I know that these are not untrue.
All my deeds so long delayed,
all the tunes I have not played
sound out on your bina's strings,
all performed by you.
I know, I know that these are counted too.

Deb

Living with uncertainty seems to me to be one of the things that poetry and entrepreneurship might have in common. Embracing it, rather than fearing it, allows for innovation and agility when confronted with an ambiguous scenario. This might be where the business takes flight or is transformed from out of the ordinary. The writing of poetry is always looking for an unexpected way of seeing something, of discarding the conventional.

Evening

The evening slowly disrobes, and hands
each garment to a row of old attendant trees.
You look on, and watch how two worlds depart –
one heaven-bound, and one which falls,

and they leave you: to your not-quite-belonging
to either – not quite as dark as the silent house,
not quite so safely given up to eternity
as the thing that becomes a star and rises each night;

and they leave you (these threads cannot be untangled)
to your life, your timid, tall and growing life,
so that – at once limited and understood –
by turns a stone is grown in you, and then a star.

Rainer Maria Rilke
Translated from the German by James Sheard

Kate

The Green Door Project founder and Mark's business coach

Kate is a qualified Business Psychologist, with over fifteen years of experience in some of the world's largest corporations, including Bupa and HSBC. In 2019, Kate launched The Green Door Project to help both individuals and organisations discover their hidden diamonds, unlock their potential and achieve the extraordinary. Kate has worked with Mark since 2021.

On listening to your body

Our bodies hold an inordinate amount of untapped intelligence, which is often referred to as somatic or embodied intelligence. It's a fascinating, rapidly developing space that offers so much potential for enhancing leadership skills and business impact. The gut–brain connection is an example that is familiar to most people – that rather queasy feeling in your stomach when a decision is slightly off or misaligned with your values. Or the uncomfortable feeling you experience when you're having lunch with a person you are considering going into partnership with, or the warm feeling you get when you've made a difference to someone's day.

Our body often registers an emotional reaction before our brain does – a racing heart, a tension headache. These can be early indicators of emotional states like anxiety or anger, and can give you data points that explain patterns of unhelpful, unresourceful and undesirable behaviours, such as why we are not always at our best, despite our efforts. Triggers are a great example of this.

Triggers are particular factors in our lives that create an emotional response that derails us from achieving our aims; for example, certain situations and behaviours. Public speaking is a very common example of this. However, triggers can absolutely be overcome, through listening to our bodies and getting underneath the reaction to work out what is triggering us and why. Once we understand what sits behind our response, we then have the opportunity to press pause and zoom out to see different perspectives and options. From here, we can rewire our thought process. In turn, this opens up the opportunity to have better control over our behaviour, decisions and outcomes.

Recognising and understanding these signals can provide hugely valuable insight, but often I find that leaders are too busy and too preoccupied with whatever their brain is telling them to give these signals the attention they deserve. The most resilient leaders I work with make a handful of highly impactful, healthy habits their non-negotiables, and are able to quickly spot the red flags that signal they are heading into overload so that they are able to course-correct.

Bath

The day is fresh-washed and fair, and there is a smell of tulips and narcissus in the air.

The sunshine pours in at the bath-room window and bores through the water in the bath-tub in lathes and planes of greenish-white. It cleaves the water into flaws like a jewel, and cracks it to bright light.

Little spots of sunshine lie on the surface of the water and dance, dance, and their reflections wobble deliciously over the ceiling; a stir of my finger sets them whirring, reeling. I move a foot and the planes of light in the water jar. I lie back and laugh, and let the green-white water, the sun-flawed beryl water, flow over me. The day is almost too bright to bear, the green water covers me from the too bright day. I will lie here awhile and play with the water and the sun spots. The sky is blue and high. A crow flaps by the window, and there is a whiff of tulips and narcissus in the air.

Amy Lowell

On managing your physical state

Learning to listen to our bodies and managing our state is a hugely powerful tool that's entirely accessible to any business leader looking to be more effective – once they can be present to the other forms of intelligence available to them.

The value of intuition

Mark and I often talk about not mistaking intuition for fact. This is important for any business leader, and there is no denying its value in business, especially for leaders who are able to access this wisdom without ego, bias and heuristics... (somewhat easier said than done).

Intuition is distinct from assumption, particularly in a psychological context. It refers to our instinctive understanding of something. It's an immediate grasp of a situation, often based on accumulated knowledge and experience. It can be argued that it's also highly reliable, especially when it comes from an expert in a field. Assumption is a belief that's accepted as true but without proof, demonstration or a solid basis. That is why untested assumptions can be considered the mother of all screw-ups (to put it politely).

The role of intuition in business, however, can have many advantages. It often comes from depth of experience and can encapsulate the complexity of situations (facts, figures, human dynamics, organisational culture, etc.) whilst rapidly making sense of them to illuminate a path forwards. It can also be a very helpful iceberg spotter when it comes to identifying risks that may be less obvious to others.

In the business world, intuition and facts are like that odd couple who don't seem to go together, but who somehow work. Intuition is the spontaneous one who makes decisions in the blink of an eye and sometimes hits the bullseye, but at other times misses the dartboard completely. Fact is the one who takes their time and analyses situations with the precision of a crime scene detective to work out what's really going on, and can turn risks into calculated moves.

They can work together in perfect harmony – the question to ask is who is leading the dance?

On Reason and Passion
(extract from 'The Prophet')

...

*Your reason and your passion are the rudder and
      the sails of your seafaring soul.
If either your sails or your rudder be broken, you can
      but toss and drift, or else be held at a standstill in mid-seas.
For reason, ruling alone, is a force confining; and passion,
      unattended, is a flame that burns to its own destruction.
Therefore let your soul exalt your reason to the height of passion,
      that it may sing;
And let it direct your passion with reason, that your passion may
      live through its own daily resurrection, and like the phoenix rise
      above its own ashes.*

...

Kahlil Gibran

2

Business as
a Nightclub

**On avoiding burnout, coping with
pressure and achieving perspective**

To A Dancing Star

Come, star, and dance with me,
You shall wear a crown of fire,
And put sudden lightning in your hair,
And leap into the great unknown
That lies beyond the skies.

Sara Teasdale

Stopping by Woods on a Snowy Evening

Whose woods these are I think I know.
His house is in the village though;
He will not see me stopping here
To watch his woods fill up with snow.

My little horse must think it queer
To stop without a farmhouse near
Between the woods and frozen lake
The darkest evening of the year.

He gives his harness bells a shake
To ask if there is some mistake.
The only other sound's the sweep
Of easy wind and downy flake.

The woods are lovely, dark and deep.
But I have promises to keep,
And miles to go before I sleep,
And miles to go before I sleep.

Robert Frost

Deb

One moment, your creative business can feel like you're flying. You're absorbed in the dance; you and the music in perfect syncopation. But too easily it can be overwhelming; the lights are flashing, the music becomes blaring and it's hard to take a breath and find your rhythm again amidst the chaos.

From Deb To Mark — Do you think you have ever been burnt out?

I didn't really think it was a thing, until I experienced it myself. What does burnout look like to you? I had really odd symptoms apart from the most obvious one of exhaustion – it felt like an almost electrical buzzing in my head. I was either working and feeling overwhelmed and scattered, or asleep... and it was only looking back that I realised I'd got through it.

What have you learnt about coping when overwhelmed by doing too much? How did you let go of some things and learn to trust others?

Thanks and love,

Deb

I get panic attacks. Bouts of anxiety. I often don't sleep well at night. For me, that's normal. My human condition. Which brings me to Kae Tempest, who Lush once hosted for a performance:

'Let Them Eat Chaos' by Kae Tempest (extract)

...

Smart flats. Rough flats.
Can't-get-enough-cat flats,
you know, seventeen cat-flaps.
Rich flats, broke flats.
New flats.
Old flats.
Luxury bespoke flats.
And this-has-got-be-a-joke flats.

Pensioners, toddlers.
Immigrants and Englishmen.
Family with six kids.
Single businesswoman.

Everybody's here trying to make or scrape a living.
The fox freezes on the alley wall and stands still, sniffing.

Bare branches sway in the front garden.
The lionmouth door knocker flaps in the breeze.
Streetlights glint on the Beware of the Dog sign.
The beer cans the crisp packets dance with the dead leaves.
It's 4:18 a.m.

At this very moment, on this very street,
seven different people in seven different flats
are wide awake.

> *Can't sleep.*

Of all of these people in all these houses,
only these seven are awake.

They shiver in the middle of the night
counting their sheepish mistakes.

...

Burnout or breakdown? Here and there. In the past, you didn't talk about it, even with friends.

But things have changed. For me there was an actual moment. An influencer called Zoella, whose first social media post was I LOVE LUSH, visited my work and we talked. After some time, the subject turned to panic attacks and I admitted to her that I had them regularly. She said I was the first person of my age who had talked freely with her about it.

That must have been around 2012. I had several techniques like the Alexander Technique to manage my panic attacks and it was difficult for people to work with me and not be aware. I first went to Kate because I couldn't cope. I wrote to Holly Tucker and said 'help'. 'What sort of help?' she asked.

Zoella and others like her have paved the way for a much kinder world – a woke culture where anxiety, panic and the neurodiverse are accepted. A multicultural world where your sexual orientation, ethnicity and all the other reasons for you to be picked on are accepted. A world I have been waiting for all my life. When I was growing up, if you had been diagnosed as autistic or were neurodiverse in any way, you were labelled.

Dylan Thomas described it brilliantly in his 1954 radio drama, 'Under Milk Wood': (extract)

WILLY NILLY   Morning, Mrs Ogmore-Pritchard.

MRS OGMORE-PRITCHARD   Good morning, postman.

WILLY NILLY   Here's a letter for you with stamped and addressed envelope enclosed, all the way from Builth Wells. A gentleman wants to study birds and can he have accommodation for two weeks and a bath, vegetarian.

MRS OGMORE-PRITCHARD   No.

WILLY NILLY   You wouldn't know he was in the
(*Persuasively*)   house, Mrs Ogmore-Pritchard. He'd be out in the mornings at the bang of dawn with his bag of breadcrumbs and his little telescope...

MRS OGMORE-PRITCHARD   And come home at all hours covered with feathers. I don't want persons in my nice clean rooms breathing all over the chairs...

WILLY NILLY	Cross my heart, he won't breathe...
MRS OGMORE-PRITCHARD	and putting their feet on my carpets and sneezing on my china and sleeping in my sheets...
WILLY NILLY	He only wants a single bed, Mrs Ogmore-Pritchard.
	[Door slams.]

I am a bird watcher, anxious and a 'vegetarian'!

Wendy Denning, my doctor, told me that most people break down in their lifetime – some people even two or three times. I think Kate differentiates between burnout and break down.

From Deb I am in a period of massive change for my tiny business.
To Mark

We are redoing everything – stock control systems, accounting, website and investigating stepping up our efficiency with manufacturing our little bottles of pills, with some help from your Nick Kendall who has introduced me to your printer there in Poole. Not quite there yet. With all of this (looking down the list of common business problems that Kate sent me), I seem to be suffering from all of the following:

Uncertainty, Scaling, Focusing on what matters, Burnout, Fear of finance, Resilience, Pressure, Ruthless prioritisation (or trying), Looking to the future, Strategy, Managing people, Listening to your body and gut, Sales...

And what is *entrepreneur's wound*? I'm sure I have that too!

Here's a poem that is going round and round in my head at the moment.

Deb

The Peace Of Wild Things

When despair for the world grows in me
and I wake in the night at the least sound
in fear of what my life and my children's lives may be,
I go and lie down where the wood drake
rests in his beauty on the water, and the great heron feeds.
I come into the peace of wild things
who do not tax their lives with forethought
of grief. I come into the presence of still water.
And I feel above me the day-blind stars
waiting with their light. For a time
I rest in the grace of the world, and am free.

Wendell Berry

John Clare was born in 1793, when anxiety and depression were misunderstood. He ended the last two decades of his life in a lunatic asylum. It's now thought that a little financial security would have saved him from that end. I prefer a business coach.

I was introduced to John Clare by Tom Hall. His bandmate Gerald from the Celebrated Ratliffe Stout Band stayed with Mo and I the night after they appeared at the Free Folk Club in Bournemouth. I never saw him again, but he left me reading and re-reading John Clare. As I was growing up, I was taught that we were heading for a cooling climate, before climate change came. I had noticed how every February the weather took a turn for the better. Upon reading 'The Shepherd's Calendar', I realised that this has been happening since the 1800s. I find reading 'The Shepherd's Calendar' a reassuring antidote to climate anxiety (don't ask why, I just do).

I love John Clare and this poem so much. It makes me smile because it, typically for you, has the air of mournful melancholy and a minor key to end on!

The Shepherd's Calendar
(extract)
…

The sun peeps through the window-pane;
Which children mark with laughing eye,
And in the wet street steal again,
To tell each other spring is nigh:
Then, as young hope the past recalls,
In playing groups they often draw,
To build beside the sunny walls
Their spring-time huts of sticks or straw.

And oft in pleasure's dreams they hie
Round homesteads by the village side,
Scratting the hedgerow mosses by
Where painted pooty shells abide;
Mistaking oft the ivy spray
For leaves that come with budding Spring,
And wond'ring, in their search for play,
Why birds delay to build and sing.
…

John Clare

On burnout

Burnout is not a place you want to find yourself in. It doesn't exactly sound inviting, but I think the reality is often worse than most people imagine. I believe many of us are in a chronic state of overload and overwhelm. Burnout is a different kettle of fish. This is when our nervous systems become stuck in fight and flight mode and no longer have the flexibility to deal with life's inevitable pressures and upsets, which are at the heart of resilience. It's not about creating a nirvana state of steady calm, as many people think, it's about our ability to experience and process upsets and recover. What it looks like is often chronic physical symptoms and an inability to engage in our normal lives, never mind business.

It can be a very long slope into burnout, yet often I work with people who say it appeared seemingly overnight. It's an even longer hill to climb back out of it. The most resilient leaders I work with are those who treat the health of their nervous systems as non-negotiable. They have a small handful of highly impactful habits that create boundaries around the things that matter to them in their life and give them energy – without these things, they know they are worse off. They might relate to sleep, exercise, quality time with family, time in nature – it's highly individual – but I see that those who are best able to handle the ebbs, flows and sometimes tsunamis of pressure, maintain their non-negotiables, especially when the pressure is on. Others, however, become too busy and let go of the very things that will sustain them.

There is so much to say on this topic, but mindset is also key in coping with circumstances around us that may be largely out of our control. We don't see the world as it is, we see the world as we are, and there is a huge amount of power in working on a mindset as a preventative of burnout and a route to happiness, despite our context. This might be about keeping things in perspective, connecting to purpose as a source of inspiration, energy and focus, seeing challenges as something to overcome rather than a threat – which as a thought alone changes the chemical released into our body. I see those who work on their mindset as more likely to stay healthy and strong amidst the pandemic of overwhelm.

I did say once to Kate: 'What if I die of overwork?'

Her reply? 'That's not your destiny.'

I had a conversation with my neighbour, John, who is nearly ninety, about retirement. He is still as active, romantic and inspiring as he has always been. He said: 'Don't retire, there's nothing to do.'

That gets you asking yourself: 'What were you planning to do?'

Today, for example, I helped plan a Lush shop. Was there something else I would have rather been doing? Not really.

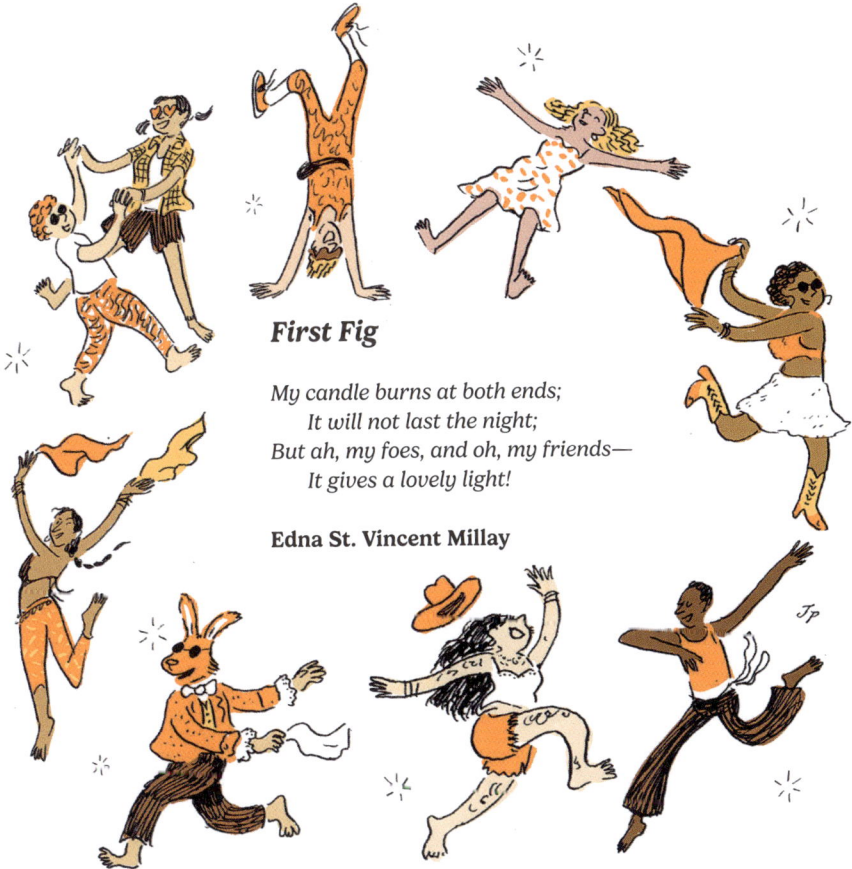

First Fig

My candle burns at both ends;
It will not last the night;
But ah, my foes, and oh, my friends—
It gives a lovely light!

Edna St. Vincent Millay

Deb

Here is a poem that I often prescribe for others, with its exhortation to 'some time make the time' to go outside, to pause in a place of limbo, an in-between space between the calm lake and the rough sea, and to allow something unexpected to happen. I like to cultivate a receptive state of creativity and possibility. This is where change comes, with creative acts and poetry – somewhere between thinking and feeling.

Postscript

And some time make the time to drive out west
Into County Clare, along the Flaggy Shore,
In September or October, when the wind
And the light are working off each other
So that the ocean on one side is wild
With foam and glitter, and inland among stones
The surface of a slate-grey lake is lit
By the earthed lightning of a flock of swans,
Their feathers roughed and ruffling, white on white,
Their fully grown headstrong-looking heads
Tucked or cresting or busy underwater.
Useless to think you'll park and capture it
More thoroughly. You are neither here nor there,
A hurry through which known and strange things pass
As big soft buffetings come at the car sideways
And catch the heart off guard and blow it open.

Seamus Heaney

On the entrepreneur's wound

An entrepreneur's wound is typically a beautiful but heartbreaking experience of hardship, or trauma, that marks defining moments in their life. These formative experiences belong in the past, but are very much alive in the present through their impact on the entrepreneur's values, beliefs, behaviours and decisions.

There are usually consequences of these experiences that are undeniably positive, such as creating the drive for extraordinary levels of achievement, but some are undeniably difficult, such as the detrimental impact they can have on mental health.

As a psychologist, working with an entrepreneur's wounds is one of the most fascinating, fulfilling and also challenging areas of my work. Understanding and acknowledging what these wounds have given leaders, whilst also understanding where these experiences no longer serve them and working through ways to transform their relationship to them. It can be an incredibly freeing experience.

When you notice you are finding things difficult, it's time to get off the dance-floor and onto the balcony of your business. To take a zoomed-out perspective of what's going on. Are you focusing on the right things? What's working well, where might you need to intervene to get something back on track, what's giving you energy, what's taking your energy away? Seeing things from that vantage point can help you focus on what matters and help you work out what needs your attention, and what you need to let go of.

3

Business as Creativity

On overcoming fear of finance,
and looking to the future

The future enters into us,
in order to transform itself in us,
long before it happens.

**Rainer Maria Rilke
from *Letters to a Young Poet***

I often see myself as walking on stepping stones across a foggy lake. I might see the next step, and the next and maybe four and five and even six after that, but I don't know the journey. If the stones are a bit wibbly-wobbly and I'm anxious, I remember to measure my life in creative acts. The more creative the acts, the happier I am.

I remember chatting to a fellow business owner once and saying to him, 'Those figures look awfully optimistic!'

And his reply was: 'I can't bear them any other way.'

Only very few types of people are asked to predict the future! The weather forecaster, astrologers and psychics and then, business owners!

Will you have rare second-hand books in your London shop?

'New Eyes Each Year' by Philip Larkin
New eyes each year
Find old books here,
And new books, too,
Old eyes renew;
So youth and age
Like ink and page
In this house join,
Minting new coin.

What made you think I had lost belief in you? Was it a poem I sent? I will not lose confidence in you.

Mark

Ah I didn't know that poem! Lovely! And the metaphor works for them poetry business beautifully! Bookshop, anthologies, poetry prescriptions and more widely, wisdom and experience speaking to new ideas...

I didn't think you had lost faith. I'm so glad and grateful, but was just in need of the reminder. You are very good at saying, 'yes you can do it'.

My back seized up last night – a trapped nerve. I believe that the body holds our stresses and strains and that it can manifest them in some way – a metaphor. I need to get moving forwards with the business now, too, and be 'majestic and free', as Wordsworth says!

I have three or four properties to go and see in central London next week...

Ready to be part of Holly Tucker's new project launch in September, too.

Thanks for everything!
Deb

We all follow Louise Hay. She says:
'Lower [back pain]; Fear of money. Lack of financial support.'

A few thoughts:

1. What feels like enough money?
2. What is a noble way of making money?
3. What are you ashamed of around money?
4. What sides of your character have stopped you making more money?

Your aphorism (also from Louise Hay):
'I trust the process of life. All I need is always taken care of. I am safe.'

A taxi driver once asked me: 'Why does a man need 900 shops?' This poem by Gibran is the answer. The well isn't overflowing – it's full. I suppose, in the end, it's all about keeping perspective and not letting the wrong thing become your aim:

Your remedy is the following poem:

From Mark
To Deb

On Giving
(extract from 'The Prophet')
...

Then said a rich man, Speak to us of Giving.
And he answered:
You give but little when you give of your possessions.
It is when you give of yourself that you truly give.
For what are your possessions but things you keep
and guard for fear you may need them tomorrow?
And tomorrow, what shall tomorrow bring to the over
prudent dog burying bones in the trackless sand as
he follows the pilgrims to the holy city?
And what is fear of need by need itself?
Is not dread of thirst when your well is full, the thirst
that is unquenchable?
...

Kahlil Gibran

Dear Kayley,

You wrote that 'the accountants and lawyers were questioning why Lush is paying for the Poetry Business School book'.

The most influential book of poems for me in business is Kahlil Gibran's 'The Prophet', where he dispenses wisdom in the guise of a seer.

For many in business, it's a dog-eat-dog world where you wouldn't wander without plenty of lawyers and accountants. I can occasionally get passionately caught up in an idea where these advisors need to represent the voice of reason.

In a section on *Buying and Selling* in 'The Prophet', Gibran points out that:

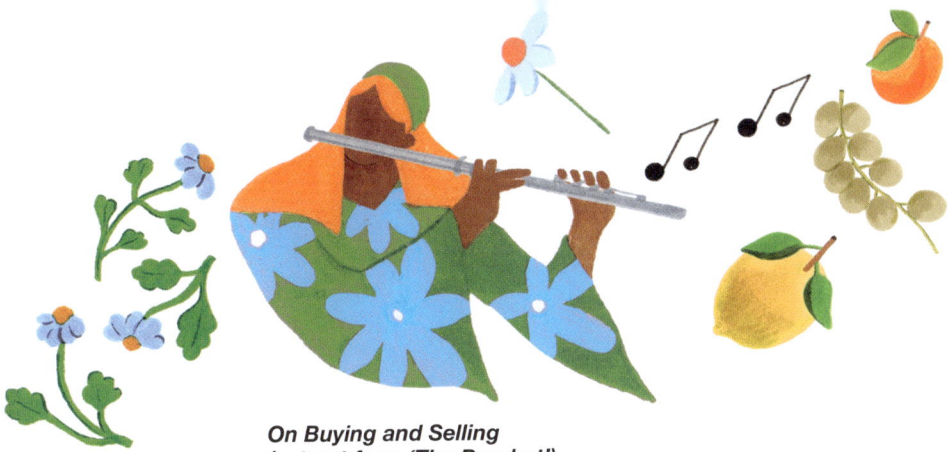

On Buying and Selling
(extract from 'The Prophet')

...

When in the market-place you toilers of the sea and fields and vineyards
    meet the weavers and the potters and the gatherers of spices –
Invoke then the master spirit of the earth, to come into your
    midst and sanctify the scales and the reckoning that weighs
    value against value.
And suffer not the barren-handed to take part in your
    transactions, who would sell their words for your labour.
To such men you should say:
'Come with us to the field, or go with our brothers to the sea
    and cast your net;
For the land and the sea shall be bountiful to you even as to us.'

And if there come the singers and the dancers and the
    flute-players – buy of their gifts also.
For they too are gatherers of fruit and frankincense, and that
    which they bring, though fashioned of dreams, is raiment
    and food for your soul.
And before you leave the market-place, see that no one has gone
    his way with empty hands.
For the master spirit of the earth shall not sleep peacefully upon
    the wind till the needs of the least of you are satisfied.

...

Kahlil Gibran

From Mark
To Deb

In Lush, we value Poets, Musicians, Artists and all those that fill our hearts with passion — their work informs and guides ours. We don't ask them to weigh their work in bath bombs any more than we would consider the lawyers and the accountants to be 'barren handed'. The best business accountants are geographers, captains of industry.

Hope that goes some way to answering your question.

Mark

From Mark
To Deb

We were talking about sales and costs recently, and I realised I had several thoughts on the subject.

It's mainly that you need to take both seriously. I have said already that one should aim to create sales to fund growth. A friend of mine with a business, for example, would sell two franchises to fund the setting up of each of his own shops. He made a few mistakes here, for example, franchising a shop in Covent Garden. I can remember his business partner looking with covetous eyes at that shop.

The problem for businesses like ours is how we enthusiastically spend everything we earn. Profit is very important if you don't wish to be doing what a rather dull banker or accountant has in mind for you.

I will look out for a good poem... 'Oh, I Wish I'd Looked After Me Teeth' by Pam Ayres comes to mind.

Left: Musicians, including the late Simon Emmerson (Lush's Music Director) inspiring an audience of Lush staff at Lushfest, Poole, 2012.

Oh, I Wish I'd Looked After Me Teeth (extract)

...

If I'd known I was paving the way
To cavities, caps and decay,
The murder of fillin's,
Injections and drillin's,
I'd have thrown all me sherbet away.

So I lie in the old dentist's chair,
And I gaze up his nose in despair,
And his drill it do whine
In these molars of mine.
'Two amalgam,' he'll say, 'for in there.'

How I laughed at my mother's false teeth,
As they foamed in the waters beneath.
But now comes the reckonin'
It's me they are beckonin'
Oh, I wish I'd looked after me teeth.

Pam Ayres

The largest single mistake we've made at Lush was to not keep a more serious eye on an area of our business which bet on the currency market just before the Lehman crash of 2008. It cost the business nineteen million pounds and years of aggravation.

From Mark To Deb

However, mistakes are made every minute of every day. If possible, don't pay heed to them. Don't give them air. The more you do, the more mistakes you make. Go through them thoroughly, though. Analyse them. Weigh them. Reach your conclusions. Be grateful you don't have a boss and carry on. Everything is negotiable — it's a mistake to think otherwise. Don't split the difference.

I think it's a mistake to focus any part of your business on shoplifters. Proper customers are 99 per cent of business - focus on them.

Focusing on products that don't sell is a mistake. Focus on the successful ones.

Try not to break someone else's rice bowl... as in don't purposely take someone's livelihood away.

When there is an opportunity to behave honourably, do it. If you can afford it, be generous. If you have made a mistake, pay up. Don't defend the indefensible - the time wasted could be used more productively. If there is no need to say something, don't.

4

Business as Neighbourhood

On working with people, and leadership

To business that we love we rise betime,
And go to 't with delight.

**William Shakespeare
from *Antony and Cleopatra***

IF

If you can keep your head when all about you
Are losing theirs and blaming it on you,
If you can trust yourself when all men doubt you,
But make allowance for their doubting too;
If you can wait and not be tired by waiting,
Or being lied about, don't deal in lies,
Or being hated, don't give way to hating,
And yet don't look too good, nor talk too wise:

If you can dream—and not make dreams your master;
If you can think—and not make thoughts your aim;
If you can meet with Triumph and Disaster
And treat those two impostors just the same;
If you can bear to hear the truth you've spoken
Twisted by knaves to make a trap for fools,
Or watch the things you gave your life to, broken,
And stoop and build 'em up with worn-out tools:

If you can make one heap of all your winnings
And risk it on one turn of pitch-and-toss,
And lose, and start again at your beginnings
And never breathe a word about your loss;
If you can force your heart and nerve and sinew
To serve your turn long after they are gone,
And so hold on when there is nothing in you
Except the Will which says to them: 'Hold on!'

If you can talk with crowds and keep your virtue,
Or walk with Kings—nor lose the common touch,
If neither foes nor loving friends can hurt you,
If all men count with you, but none too much;
If you can fill the unforgiving minute
With sixty seconds' worth of distance run,
Yours is the Earth and everything that's in it,
And—which is more—you'll be a Man, my son!

Rudyard Kipling

Deb

Successful businesses often see themselves as working in collaboration, and envisage themselves as part of a neighbourhood where relationships are fostered, which transcend transactional exchanges.

From Mark
To Deb

I was in Canada when a recipient of Lush's Charity Pot[1] funding said that she saw the Lush shops as an 'oasis of kindness'. Obviously we liked this idea, and it's another of our aims. We also like the idea of making the world Lusher than we found it.

For a while at Marks & Spencer, staff (supposedly) couldn't grow a beard. They can't do this, can't do that… Why is Lush such a good employer? We employ people who are self-determining, opinionated, vegans, activists and free-thinkers. We encourage Random Acts of Kindness.

We are trying to behave ourselves while everyone else seems to lie and cheat! This will be the business we want it to be.

If you can keep your head when all about you
         Are losing theirs and blaming it on you,
If you can trust yourself when all men doubt you,
         But make allowance for their doubting too;

I've been lauded as a leader in business for at least thirty years and it's all to do with Kipling's 'If':

If you can meet with Triumph and Disaster
         And treat those two impostors just the same

This runs so deep in me; it means everything to me.

[1]*Lush Charity Pot – body lotion and 100 per cent of its sales, minus government taxes, goes into the Charity Pot fund which supports small-scale organisations and campaigners in the areas of animal protection, human rights and the environment.*

If through finding your voice

If through finding your voice
They lose theirs
You have not found your voice

If through making your choice
They lose theirs
Have you made the right choice?

If by claiming your power
They become powerless
Are you really strong?

If by asserting your position
They lose theirs
Do you really belong?

Kate Jenkinson

It's Christmas time, Deb! Time for Peter Pan and Tinker Bell...
When we were last speaking on the phone, you had to go and say:
'You can have too much of a good thing' and 'bloody poems!'

From Mark
To Deb

When you say things like that, just like with not believing in fairies, poets die.

I had met the late Benjamin Zephaniah a few times. He performed with The Imagined Village[2] and had also joined us at Lush parties where he recited his wonderful work. He told us he liked our vegetarian principles and liked that we had vegan food at the parties. His principles and ours aligned and it felt good.

I particularly remember this Christmas poem where at its end I felt guilty for making 'loadsa cash' from Christmas:

[2] Formed in 2004 by Simon Emmerson and featuring a stellar cast of musicians from a wide variety of ethnic and cultural backgrounds, The Imagined Village came together to create folk music that represented modern multiculturalism in the UK. In his role creating soundtracks for the Lush Spa, Simon brought many Imagined Village musicians along, blending their talents into the Spa's unique soundscapes.

Talking Turkeys!!!
(extract)
...

I once knew a turkey called… Turkey
He said 'Benji explain to me please,
Who put de turkey in christmas
An what happens to christmas trees?'
I said 'I am not too sure turkey
But it's nothing to do wid Christ Mass
Humans get greedy an waste more dan need be
An business men mek loadsa cash.'

Be nice to yu turkey dis christmas
Invite dem indoors fe sum greens
Let dem eat cake an let dem partake
In a plate of organic grown beans,
Be nice to yu turkey dis christmas
An spare dem de cut of de knife,
Join Turkeys United an dey'll be delighted
An yu will mek new friends 'FOR LIFE'.

Benjamin Zephaniah

Such sad news. Benjamin was very loved although I never met him. Lots of friends are very sad today. I'm so glad that you knew him and that he had these links with Lush! I'm sorry you lost a friend in him.

On the train to London now. I have to read a lot of poetry and still every day, one will shine a light through the rest and remind me of what it can do… I retract my earlier negative statements.

See you tomorrow!
D

Time for action, I think?

I've made an arrangement with our Collabs team for you to open in their shop in the front of our offices in Beak Street, London, for November and December, if that is something you would like to do?

That way you can have a little try. We will pay for the fit out… you give us a percentage of the takings. You get a showroom for the landlords to visit and hopefully your partner Jim will like it.

Of course, you will have Lush fans to contend with.

Dear Mark,

Still here in Valletta in Malta at the moment, looking out over the beautiful city at night. Back on Tuesday.

This is an exciting and extraordinary offer.

Don't quite know what to say…

I'd love to see you when you're next in London maybe… too much to say and ask in an email.

Do let me know when you're there?

Love Deb

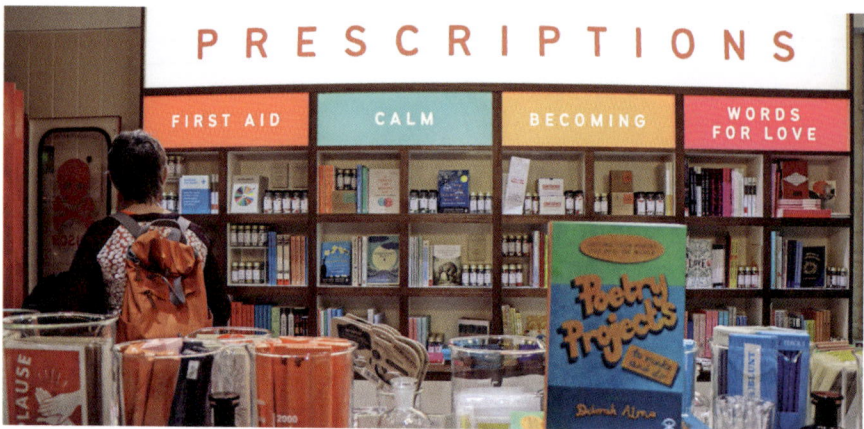

Above: Poetry Pharmacy's pop-up open for business in Lush Studio Soho, London, 2023.

From Mark
To Deb

Dear Deb,

It is exciting to see your Poetry Pharmacy pop-up shop coming together. Only a matter of days.

I was talking to Kate today and a regular issue came up.

Kate doesn't like it when I use going quiet as a management technique. I use it a lot.

I'm not really sure why she doesn't like it – after all, it's a fairly gentle thing. On the whole, I am in favour of doing *something*. It was my accountant from my Cosmetics to Go[3] days who would encourage me to add time to a situation. It's not a common practice, and I really don't think I have it right. There is something antagonistic about just disappearing – if you don't have a solution to a situation, it can be preferable to blundering on. Is leaving others to consider their own actions kinder than lecturing or hectoring them? Or is it just leaving them to stew? It isn't only them stewing though. You also have time to consider.

In my case, I go birding. If I am falling out with someone, I prefer going birding to having an argument with them. However, if forced to face up to a situation, I do believe that argument uncovers the correct path forward and it is certainly the pathway to creative solutions. Anyway, despite a lot of coaching, I still go silent on people. Given an opportunity, I would prefer to find a poem and add someone else's wisdom to my argument. The problem is that once you accept that you are often wrong, giving a situation plenty of thought is preferable to making a mistake.

The folllowing poem is obliquely about succession and destiny; a child's thoughts on their parents. It's also especially about charm, charisma and power over others:

[3] Founded in 1988 by a team of eventual Lush co-founders, Cosmetics To Go blazed a trail through the cosmetics industry until 1994. Today, many Cosmetics To Go products, ideas and staff have made their way into Lush.

I Need Not Go

I need not go
Through sleet and snow
To where I know
She waits for me;
She will wait me there
Till I find it fair,
And have time to spare
From company.

When I've overgot
The world somewhat,
When things cost not
Such stress and strain,
Is soon enough
By cypress sough
To tell my Love
I am come again.

And if some day,
When none cries nay,
I still delay
To seek her side,
(Though ample measure
Of fitting leisure
Await my pleasure)
She will not chide.

What—not upbraid me
That I delayed me,
Nor ask what stayed me
So long? Ah, no! –
Now cares may claim me,
New loves inflame me,
She will not blame me,
But suffer it so.

Thomas Hardy

On leaning in

It's less about not liking going quiet as a management technique, and more about questioning whether as a default it is going to achieve the best possible outcomes in the best possible way! I'm not a fan of blanket approaches. I think it's about always asking questions – what do I really want to achieve here? What's the best way to get to that outcome?

I don't disagree with being thoughtful in our responses, quite the opposite. However, when you notice patterns that might suggest habit and not thought, it might be time to ask what sits behind that response? What am I trying to avoid? Is there a fear that may be keeping me (and others) stuck or holding us back? In my experience, 'leaning in' often requires courage to step through these fears, which usually pays dividends.

Ask Me

Some time when the river is ice ask me
mistakes I have made. Ask me whether
what I have done is my life. Others
have come in their slow way into
my thought, and some have tried to help
or to hurt: ask me what difference
their strongest love or hate has made.

I will listen to what you say.
You and I can turn and look
at the silent river and wait. We know
the current is there, hidden; and there
are comings and goings from miles away
that hold the stillness exactly before us.
What the river says, that is what I say.

William Stafford

On human connection

It's hard to sum up what makes a good working environment because, to a degree, it's context specific. What works well for Google will not necessarily work well in the military, and vice versa. However, if I take it to what may be uniformly true, then one of the major aspects I would highlight is the quality of human connection, and the ability to meet the human needs that allow people to be at their best.

Psychological safety has had a lot of press in recent years and it is critical to unlocking the innovation required for businesses to adapt, evolve and grow. How does a leader do this? There are a number of ways, but one I think is particularly powerful is by showing vulnerability. This creates trust and that leads to psychological safety.

One of the attributes that sits behind the ability to do this, and distinguishes great leaders from good leaders, is humility – a leader who is about the business, not about ego. One who is connected to purpose, who both leads and inspires others from this purpose rather than the need for a personal win. One who helps others find meaning and belonging in their work. It's not about the 'I' but instead the focus is on the 'we' (a sense of the collective) and the 'it'. This doesn't mean that ambition can't exist in a humble leader – it absolutely can. It is a paradoxical mix of deep personal humility and intense professional ambition – a very powerful alchemy. I see Mark as someone with these leadership attributes and as an inspiring example of how impactful they are.

Dear Deb,

I'm not sure about this humility thing. A friend of mine was a mendicant Anglican friar working in a hospice. Being a devotee, he could never understand why folk weren't keen on dying. After all, they were going to meet their maker and that was surely exciting. One day, worn down by it all, he called me. 'Oh Mark,' he said, 'this f—king humility is really getting me down.'

At work recently, we were talking about being hippies. We wondered who the ultimate hippy was and decided it was Jesus. Then when we started asking 'what would Jesus do in this situation?'

'Ha!' I always say to myself, 'What would Jesus do?!'
But he's a hard act to follow...
D

5

Business as a Garden

On growth, scaling-up and ruthless prioritising

Engineers' Corner

Why isn't there an Engineers' Corner in Westminster Abbey?
 In Britain we've always made more fuss of a ballad than a blueprint
. . . How many schoolchildren dream of becoming great engineers?
            Advertisement placed in *The Times* by the Engineering Council

We make more fuss of ballads than of blueprints –
That's why so many poets end up rich,
While engineers scrape by in cheerless garrets.
Who needs a bridge or dam? Who needs a ditch?

Whereas the person who can write a sonnet
Has got it made. It's always been the way,
For everybody knows that we need poems
And everybody reads them every day.

Yes, life is hard if you choose engineering –
You're sure to need another job as well;
You'll have to plan your projects in the evenings
Instead of going out. It must be hell.

While well-heeled poets ride around in Daimlers,
You'll burn the midnight oil to earn a crust,
With no hope of a statue in the Abbey,
With no hope, even, of a modest bust.

No wonder small boys dream of writing couplets
And spurn the bike, the lorry and the train.
There's far too much encouragement for poets –
That's why this country's going down the drain.

Wendy Cope

Deb

In business, tending to growth has obvious parallels with a thoughtful gardener; the careful cultivation, attention to detail, some patience, to sowing the seeds of success, and then hopefully reaping the fruits of your labour.

From Deb
To Mark

Dear Mark,

I'm just back from a couple of days exploring a bit of Dorset with Jim in our little campervan, which was, as it happened, a really useful time to mull over what me and you had discussed in Poole on Thursday. It was very inspiring, energising and overwhelming to see lovely Lush and its mock-up shops and new ventures, and to speak to some of the people who have been there from the beginning. Everyone was so lovely and welcoming to me.

I appreciate the enormous value in being supported and mentored in this way – it's the most extraordinary thing and too valuable to do anything but rise to the challenge, however terrifying it may be.

The step to buy this Poetry Pharmacy in Bishop's Castle (a mixed residential/commercial premises) felt like an experiment, but, for me at least, not at all risky. I knew the way out, and any improvements to the shop were adding to the asset of the building it's in.

This feels different, and would need conventional borrowing if we were to take on a significant rental in London, employ and train staff, and invest in larger-scale production and supply. So, we are going to look at our figures and talk to some lenders and see where this takes us...

The poem then? For reassurance, or fear of the unknown? Here's a poem that I might recommend to myself!

Lovely to see you all and thank you so much for believing in the Poetry Pharmacy as an idea!

Love Deb

You Reading This, Be Ready

Starting here, what do you want to remember?
How sunlight creeps along a shining floor?
What scent of old wood hovers, what softened
sound from outside fills the air?

Will you ever bring a better gift for the world
than the breathing respect that you carry
wherever you go right now? Are you waiting
for time to show you some better thoughts?

When you turn around, starting here, lift this
new glimpse that you found; carry into evening
all that you want from this day. This interval you spent
reading or hearing this, keep it for life—

What can anyone give you greater than now,
starting here, right in this room, when you turn around?

William Stafford

In the spirit of this book and this generous mentorship from you, here's where we're at...

These last few days, I viewed a potential shop in Seven Dials, met a really lovely man, James Burt, from a lettings agency that does some work for Lush, and I was then really surprised by the almost complete overlooking of poetry at the London Book Fair and within the Booksellers Association. I'm used to being overlooked because I'm talking about poetry – I watch people's eyes glaze over, until I tell them how I do it...

I went from that to a meeting with you where you are taking my left-field business idea seriously and I feel enormously empowered and encouraged by that. I feel like I want to take on the establishment of the book trade and show them that poetry can be for everyone and has something to say. That it can sell. I like being enraged and turning it into action!

Then one night came both the ideas and the hurdles to overcome. I want to divide the shop into sections of clear emotional states, and we need to develop our own products to explain these sections. So I have products to develop, products to make in quantity, and a shop in London to look for...

I think, Mark, you spoke of not expecting to make any profit for two years, but we're already three years in and only just out of being 'new' and only just slowing putting all the money back into the business. I don't think we can do that for another two years, and a London shop is a huge stretch already. I feel over-faced by the prospect of being inside Covent Garden market itself. I don't feel this way about Seven Dials – I feel excited. I believe that people will find us, but you're right, it does need to be passing trade and tourists too. I feel quite confident that we'll get some attention from the press when we open, though, coupled with interest generated by your mentorship and the book.

Anyway, it was very lovely to see you and I loved so much that you and your fellow co-founders are all there in the place you started, family and colleagues popping in — it feels very like here! I hope one day you'll see it!

And the poem?

Lots of love

Deb

This (edited!) poem teaches you that patience when getting a London shop is no virtue:

From Mark
To Deb

'London, 1802' by William Wordsworth (extract)

London hath need of thee: she is a fen
Of stagnant waters: altar, sword, and pen,
Fireside, the heroic wealth of hall and bower,
Have forfeited their ancient English dower
Of inward happiness. We are selfish men;
Oh! raise us up, return to us again;
And give us manners, virtue, freedom, power.
Thy soul was like a Star, and dwelt apart:
Thou hadst a voice whose sound was like the sea:
Pure as the naked heavens, majestic, free,

Get six shop enquiries going. When they tell you that they are deciding between you and something crap, tell them you have several other shops that you're looking at. This is not the time for patience. After all, London needs *thee: she is a fen.*

Mark

We talked of 'the real world' and how we all want someone to create a place where we feel safe, even if we know the hook on the shutters doesn't work. When you choose Seven Dials, you sort of agree with the organisers of the London Book Fair. Do you believe that poetry isn't mainstream enough to be in a busy location like the piazza in Covent Garden? In the end you must make the decision... but without permanent intentions, you have absolutely no protection. When are people shopping in Seven Dials? Go there before 12pm and even then there is nothing to draw them there. If you want to rely on people finding you, I think you already have the right location.

I think we are going to have to go shopping in London together.

Hello Mark,

I'm going to have a look at this small-ish shop on Silver Place.

I think it's a good spot... a development from the pop-up. Poetry Pharmacy will also be at London Book Fair, so let's see what happens and then plan something bigger after that?

I must admit, I like a few people about. Call me old fashioned, but how do you stay in business in places like Silver Place? Years ago, Kiehl's had a shop in Bath on Quiet Street. I think I mentioned it was always great fun to go and stand in it at Christmas and tell the staff how peaceful it was. Anyway, they moved to a busier part of town.

From Mark
To Deb

Don't know if I mentioned it, Deb, but I work with many top-class retailers and you are one of the best. You question why I bother to help? It's just that you deserve a bigger audience and you aren't going to find it in Silver Place.

To change the mood a little – I have Covid. It's winter, and I was given a beautiful collection of Thomas Hardy's poetry for Christmas. I mentioned before that my grandfather had a shop in South Street in Dorchester that Hardy frequented. I courted my wife Mo in Dorchester in the seventies. A couple of weeks ago, Mo and I went to visit with our friends Jeff and Geri. We were looking for my grandfather's unmarked grave in a graveyard; unmarked because my grandmother wanted none of their children to visit him! What could he have done to cause such an act as to leave his grave unmarked? Mum said they only ever argued about the shop. He was a workaholic, she said, and wanted his daughters and wife to work in it. Mum's two sisters never did. Mum was only eight when he died. Why was my nan so cross with him?

I have sent you this poem before, I know, but it resonates, especially today:

The Going

Why did you give no hint that night
That quickly after the morrow's dawn,
And calmly, as if indifferent quite,
You would close your term here, up and be gone
    Where I could not follow
    With wing of swallow
To gain one glimpse of you ever anon!

    Never to bid good-bye
    Or lip me the softest call,
Or utter a wish for a word, while I
Saw morning harden upon the wall,
    Unmoved, unknowing
    That your great going
Had place that moment, and altered all.

Why do you make me leave the house
And think for a breath it is you I see
At the end of the alley of bending boughs
Where so often at dusk you used to be;
    Till in darkening dankness
    The yawning blankness
Of the perspective sickens me!

You were she who abode
    By those red-veined rocks far West,
You were the swan-necked one who rode
Along the beetling Beeny Crest,
    And, reining nigh me,
    Would muse and eye me,
While Life unrolled us its very best.

Why, then, latterly did we not speak,
Did we not think of those days long dead,
And ere your vanishing strive to seek
That time's renewal? We might have said,
    'In this bright spring weather
    We'll visit together
Those places that once we visited.'

    Well, well! All's past amend,
        Unchangeable. It must go.
I seem but a dead man held on end
To sink down soon. . . . O you could not know
        That such swift fleeing
        No soul foreseeing–
Not even I–would undo me so!

Thomas Hardy

**From Deb
To Mark**

So sorry to hear that you have had Covid! Mo too? I really hope it wasn't too bad and that you're back to full strength?

Thanks as always for your words and the poem – I know, I know... I am utterly convinced, but....

Silver Place is out the front door of Lush Studio Soho on Beak Street, turn left and it's the pedestrianised street a few hundred yards along. Right in the heart of Soho. I spoke to a woman from Soho Radio and local residents are really keen to have another bookshop that sells new books. It also has a small outside courtyard. It appeals to me as the next step... and then the big bastard brave place after that, after I've some money in my pocket to do it. I'll look at it anyway. It doesn't preclude me later taking a bigger shop in central London.

I will do this, but we have £30,000 in the bank, no ability to borrow against the business, and a crap mortgage here that's about to go up. Opening a bookshop needs £50,000 at least and I'm going to do it in the face of, for me, eye-watering rents and only £30,000. I'm resourceful. I can do it, but fitting a slightly bigger place is beyond me at the moment, and I want to do it well. You have been amazing and supportive and helped me beyond any hope or expectation, but I can't see a way to go for the busy central London spaces at the moment.

The London Book Fair will spark all sorts of things, I think.

Now I must get on with that book!

Deb,

Do you run for trains?

Why do you need a poem that says 'Get on with it'?

A friend whose husband died of malaria said to me:
'If we'd known what we were rushing towards, we wouldn't have been in such a hurry.'

You have a few minor issues:
1. You believe you don't have enough money to get a good position.
2. Your partner is worried.
3. You have a strong image of the type of shop you should go for and where.
4. The pop-up is ending.

Are there some others?

Hello Mark,

On the train on my way to Beak Street to see the team there and Gina and Matt to talk about the book, but yes, I guess that just about sums it up.

I think I can do it resourcefully. I needed a poem from you that speaks of confidence and action to fit into the book way back in our conversation when I wasn't even taking the idea seriously!

Tomorrow I'm speaking at a small publisher's festival about our collaboration! Lots of interest out there!

Love Deb

I would like to add Napoleon's famous quote alongside my Hardy poem recommendation: 'Never interrupt your enemy when he is making a mistake.'

In that instance, Napoleon was supposed to have said this as he was laying out his forces before battle. I have used it a lot when being confronted with difficult or seemingly insurmountable situations. It's a very French thing. When first negotiated in France, I learnt a lot. For example, we would negotiate a deal in typical Anglo-Saxon style, going through each progressive stage to end up signing a negotiated lease or partnership or licence. Then at the end, my French counterpart would start again at the beginning. What? But now the other side knew all my points as they unfolded. It could happen three times before, exasperated, I would give up. It is partly responsible for the charm of France. The slower pace and belief in conversation over action. I am aware of it now and quite like it. The worst aspect of negotiating in Britain is the principle of splitting the difference — it's a classic way of making a mistake.

To put it another way; making sure your London shop is in the right location and deserves your time and consideration. It is not the preserve of a landlord and will say a lot about your belief in your concept. Location, location, location.

Mark

From Deb
To Mark

Thank you, Mark. I **am** listening. I contacted the Shaftesbury estate again and asked them to come and take a look at the pop-up and see just how sweet-shop lovely it is in the flesh. They are going to meet me there and maybe something will come of that?

I am learning about whether it should be a Poetry Pharmacy 'proper' (like a Boots chemist with consultation rooms and a pharmacy counter), or a condensed version like the pop-up (like a Boots at the airport)? We can be flexible and respond to our location and the building, so I've been uncertain as to which way to go. The pop-up will help me with this...

Love and thanks as ever,

Deb

I do need to honour my new creative partner in business and life, ChatGPT, who worked tirelessly with me on the following poem. It reminds me of your journey to find your next home, Debs.

We had a few prototypes in the beginning which weren't quite right, but after a few rounds of iterations, we landed here. I thought it was pretty good!

Sadly, I can take no credit for the fact that ChatGPT scans!

We did a little work early this morning on another poem that I think reflects the process of experimenting in order to find something beautiful.

Ha! I guess it's fed with wisdom and insight, it's a useful tool in your hands! I have been playing with it too and it's terrible if you try to force it not to rhyme! Hope to see you sooner or later, Kate, it's been ages. Love and thanks for your kind words.
Deb

In the lab where dreams take flight,
Through the lens of starry night,
Every test, a journey new,
Seeking truths, both false and true.

With each trial, the mind refines,
Through the maze of countless signs,
Mistakes whisper, lessons learned,
In the fires where passion burned.

Alchemist in white attire,
Mixing elements with fire,
Crafting futures, bold and bright,

In the crucible of light.

For perfection's not a state,
But a path we navigate,
Through experiments, we roam,
Finding eventually, our home.

Iterations, like a dance,
Giving every dream a chance,
In each failure, wisdom's seed,
In each success, a creed.

So we test, and thus we grow,
In the lab's fluorescent glow,
Seeking what's both wonderful and true,
In this endless quest anew.

Kate Downey-Evans & ChatGPT

**From Deb
To Mark**

Hello Mark,

Hope all is well with you?

I was so sorry to hear of the end of the Body Shop recently. I was one of the young women who felt inspired by its ideas and products in the late 1970s/1980s and have enjoyed some of your stories about your time there with the Body Shop and your relationship with Anita Roddick. I'm sorry if it's a sad time for you? Great article in *The Times*!

**From Mark
To Deb**

Dear Deb,

Anita was a dynamo. Restless.

She was creative and intuitive and infuriating. But in the end, I am left with the impression of vulnerability.

I once asked her if she were an animal, what would it be? She said a female deer, or a doe. She was sure she would die young and lived life accordingly.

I said in *The Times* opinion piece that I learnt a lot from her. You ask 'what?' I think it is that things matter less than you thought they did. It's also that words are important. They mean so much that people go over them repeatedly trying to find meaning. Does this matter in business? Whether you are trying to describe your product to a potential customer or a backer, or inspire a colleague to follow your lead, you are always struggling to get your message across in a way that is honest, inspiring and true. That's why poetry is an important tool. It's emotional communication at its finest. So is good business.

Too Heavy

Dear Doctor,
I am writing to complain about these words
you have given me, that I carry in my bag
lymphatic, nodal, progressive, metastatic

They must be made of lead. I haul them everywhere.
I've cricked my neck, I'm bent
with the weight of them
palliative, metabolic, recurrent.

And when I get them out and put them on the table
they tick like bombs and overpower my own
sweet tasting words
orange, bus, coffee, June

I've been leaving them
crumpled up in pedal bins
where they fester and complain.
diamorphine, biopsy, inflammatory

And then you say
Where are your words Mrs Patient?
What have you done with your words?

Or worse, you give me that dewy look
Poor Mrs Patient has lost all her words, but shush,
don't upset her. I've got spares in the files.
Thank god for files.

So I was wondering,
Dear Doctor, if I could have
a locker
with a key.
I could collect them
one at a time,
and lay them on a plate
morphine-based, diagnostically,

with a garnish of
lollypop, monkey, lip.

Julia Darling

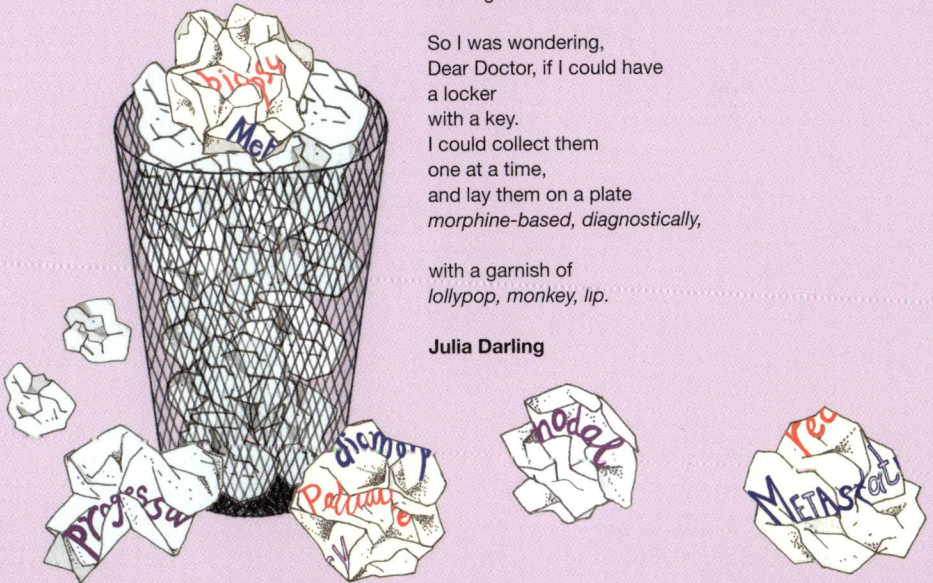

I made a decision today, and you may not approve, but I'm making an offer on a shop in Silver Place.

I know you think it's quiet there. Here are my reasons!

It's in the heart of Soho, it's a thoroughfare, it's picturesque, it's in great condition, and it's easy for Poetry Pharmacy to occupy quickly.

It's 200 yards away from our good friends at Lush, and all that Lush means to me and Maya, for whom this is no small task to take on.

It feels like a good compromise to me between your big ambitions for the Poetry Pharmacy and Jim's fear of financial ruin, destitution and being tied to the yoke of working until his teeth fall out...

It does not preclude another larger collaborative enterprise somewhere bigger and bolder – I do want to still do that. Maybe Charing Cross Road, Covent Garden...

It's our next step and it's a bold one for us. I liked the feel of the building in Silver Place, its wooden floors, its courtyard in the middle of Soho, its functioning loo...

Deb

I talked to all of the property folk at my end – they don't recommend Silver Place.

I recently went to the dentist. It was a big piece of work. I told him afterwards that there are some words you never want to hear pass a dentist's lips, and 'chisel', 'mallet' and 'sutures' are amongst them.

Anita and I once had an argument on the phone. She called me unprofessional. Now I can't even remember why. I was indignant. We argued. Eventually she asked if it was all right if she called me a wanker. Yes, I said, it was alright. I didn't mind that, but she couldn't call me unprofessional. An hour later there was a knock on my door. A delivery man with a huge bunch of flowers. He had a smirk on his face and when I opened the card that came with the flowers, I could see why. The message?

'Wanker.'

PS The useful advice I got from Anita and Gordon on scaling up was to get good financial help early. As to filling lots of little poetry pill capsules? You will work that out for yourself.

Dear Deb,

Business and death.

To carry on with the Anita and The Body Shop thread, I was twenty-five when I met her. So many of us collaborated to build that business. I can remember so vividly my first trip to Canada in January 1981 when I met Margot, her husband Quig and her sister Betty Anne. They were so impressive as they went about opening shops and dealing with the business of building the Canadian Body Shop. Last night, it went into receivership.

Businesses have lives. Warren Buffett and Charlie Munger of legendary investment company Berkshire Hathaway have been so successful investing in companies with long lives like their own. A public company's average lifetime is twenty-five years, and a family company's is forty or fifty. Buffett and Munger also specialised in keeping people working into their nineties. Munger himself died in November 2023, aged ninety-nine.

6
Business as a Journey

On taking risks and authenticity

On This Wondrous Sea
(extract)

On this wondrous sea
Sailing silently
Ho!, pilot, Ho!
Knows thou the shore
Where no breakers roar—
Where the storm is o'er?

Emily Dickinson

A ship in harbour is safe, but that
is not what ships are built for.

John Augustus Shedd

The door

Go and open the door.
  Maybe outside there's
  a tree, or a wood,
  a garden,
  or a magic city.

Go and open the door.
  Maybe a dog's rummaging,
  Maybe you'll see a face,
or an eye,
or the picture
          of a picture.

Go and open the door.
  If there's a fog
  it will clear.

Go and open the door.
  Even if there's only
  the darkness ticking,
  even if there's only
  the hollow wind,
  even if
          nothing
                is there,
go and open the door.

At least
there'll be
a draught.

Miroslav Holub
Translated from the Czech by Ian Milner

Dear Deb,

The point is, we have to sail.

You think that because Lush has been a success, I think anyone can be a success
– is that what is worrying you?

You never lose your own judgement, and no theory or friend's recommendations
should persuade you against your own judgement.

Lush have just opened in Covent Garden. It's expensive.
The accountants weren't sure and did depressing 'what-ifs'.
We took it. It's making twenty per cent more than anticipated.

'Faint Heart Never Won Fair Lady' by Sir John Bowring
(extract)

He who is both brave and bold
Wins the lady that he would;
But the courageless and cold
Never did and never could.

Regarding landlords, remember:
'**Everything** is negotiable. Whether or not the negotiation is easy is another thing.'
Carrie Fisher

Here are some lines borrowed from William Wordsworth's
'I Wandered Lonely as a Cloud'...

'Wordsworth in Covent Garden!'

I wandered lonely as a cloud
That floats on high o'er vales and hills,
When all at once I saw a crowd,

They stretched in never-ending line
Along the margin of a bay:
Ten thousand saw I at a glance,
Tossing their heads in sprightly dance.

The waves beside them danced; but they
Out-did the sparkling waves in glee:
A poet could not but be gay,
In such a jocund company:
I gazed – and gazed – but little thought
What wealth the show to me had brought:

For oft, when on my couch I lie
In vacant or in pensive mood,
They flash upon that inward eye
Which is the bliss of solitude;
And then my heart with pleasure fills,
And dances with the ringing tills.

Mark

From Mark
To Deb

When our previous business entered receivership, it was shaming. Seventeen successful years of business ended with Lloyds putting one of their most alpha male bankers in charge of our account and him telling me, amongst other things, how arrogant he thought I was and that they wanted their money back. That was followed by us talking exclusively to Next, who, having gone through all our figures, told us our business was a 'crock of sh–t' and proceeded to open five Bath & Body Works instead.

Then came the receivers, who fired us all and built a fee for themselves that was twenty times bigger than the one we had agreed with them while we were employed. The final ignominy came when I had to take full responsibility for it all and sign the final papers at the official receivers. When that was done, I offered the receiver my handshake and he refused to take it.

You ask what I am afraid of? All of that.

The Weighing

The heart's reasons
seen clearly,
even the hardest
will carry
its whip-marks and sadness
and must be forgiven.

As the drought-starved
eland forgives
the drought-starved lion
who finally takes her,
enters willingly then
the life she cannot refuse,
and is lion, is fed,
and does not remember the other.

So few grains of happiness
measured against all the dark
and still the scales balance.

The world asks of us
only the strength we have and we give it.
Then it asks more, and we give it.

Jane Hirshfield

From Mark
To Deb

You ask if I need a prescription to increase my confidence? Always.

However, you were kind enough to send me some poetry pills a month or two ago and I haven't taken them. I took a few this morning and the excerpt from 'The Weighing' jumped out at me.

Weighing is the sh-tty end of the business management stick, isn't it?

That's the way of poetry – there's no simple answer. It asks more of you; you have to think about it.

Some of the current problems in my own business were caused by lack of confidence upon starting again. I have always liked working in successful teams, but that made this trait far worse. I've told my story, but each of us in Cosmetics to Go had a severe series of moments when the world asked for more and none of us could give it.

From Deb
To Mark

We won the 2024 Midlands Bookseller of the Year award!

Embargoed for now!

From Mark
To Deb

Did you put poetry into the London Book Fair just as you planned?

Mark, it was extraordinary! Not just poetry in the Book Fair, but we were the most beautiful space. It felt like everyone who visited wanted to work with us in some way. Trying to make sense of it.

*Above: Poetry Pharmacy at the London Book Fair, March 2024.
Deb and Maya Rowland speaking to visitors to the stand.*

Mrs Dalloway
(extract)

In people's eyes, in the swing, tramp, and trudge;
in the bellow and the uproar;
the carriages, motorcars, omnibuses, vans,
sandwich men shuffling and swinging;
brass bands; barrel organs;
in the triumph and the jingle and the strange high singing
of some aeroplane overhead
was what she loved;
life; London; this moment of June.

Virginia Woolf

Would you like to have the Poetry Pharmacy, including a café, on the first floor at the front of our Oxford Street store?

It's just a suggestion from my daughter Claire.

Blimey! Blimey! Well of course I'd love that... it's extraordinary! I'd be a fool...

I think I need to speak to you. Happy to come down to Poole for this one, or online or phone call, but so many questions and I still want to open our own standalone Poetry Pharmacy in London in time. I know that interests us both.

Other collaborations are so much more likely with this too. Anyway, let me know when I can find you.

I was in the middle of composing a long email to you and here's a beautiful bomb in the middle of that!

Love Deb

In my head, your Oxford Street concession is only a stepping stone:

From Mark
To Deb

'Poem Without Ends' by Alastair Reid

One cannot take the beginning out of the air
saying 'It is the time: the hour is here'.
The process is continuous as wind,
the bird observed, not rising, but in flight,
unrealised, in motion of the mind.

The end of everything is similar, never
actually happening, but always over.
The agony, the bent head, only tell
that already in the heart the innocent evening
is thick with the ferment of farewell.

From Deb
To Mark

Following the London Book Fair, we are speaking to several international booksellers and distributors. We'll see if anything comes of it...

I'm so delighted to have been offered a publishing deal with Macmillan to edit a set of eight anthologies which match our 'sections' in the Poetry Pharmacy![4]

And following our win as Midland Regional Winner for Bookseller of the Year, we are now up against the other regional winners for National Bookseller of the Year. This involves a posh event in London - much anguish here about What To Wear.
D

Mark
I'm sure everything will go swimmingly tonight!

Deb
Thanks so much Mark! Love and gratitude to you! Mentioned our book on BBC Radio London just now too. See you soon!

Mark
The opening went well?

Deb
It was a triumph! Lots to tell you about.

Mark
Want to hear all the exciting news.

[4] A collaborative publishing agreement was also later reached between Lush and HarperCollins*Publishers* to publish *The Poetry Business School* in 2025.

Above: Poetry Pharmacy's concession launches in Lush Spa Oxford St, London, 31 May 2024.

Above: Deb celebrates the launch of the Poetry Pharmacy concession in Lush Spa Oxford Street, London, 31 May 2024.

Deb

I didn't write to Mark for the first three weeks after we opened in Lush Oxford Street as it was very quiet. Jim and I sat and re-watched the whole of *Game of Thrones* in the evenings after working hard all day in order to escape from our daily reality, which was watching ourselves sink into debt as we weren't turning over enough to cover our staffing costs. At least things weren't as bad as being roasted by the fiery breath of dragons.

Then we were discovered by Georgie Mortimer, Executive Editor at Secret London, *the ultra-shareable online guide to news, events and things to do in London*, who wrote an article about us opening in Lush Oxford Street. Then they came and made a lovely video, which was widely shared on social media. We went viral, with millions of views. People heard about us and visited, and loved us and made their own videos, which they shared, and on it went. Our daily sales initially went up massively, then settled down to a rate that meant we were a success. I'm writing this just two months in, and I think it's working!

> **Deb**
> It's absolutely extraordinary! You were right!

> **Mark**
> Of course. Did you doubt me?

> **Deb**
> Um… didn't think it would be so busy! It's mainly our own products that we're selling!

> **Mark**
> Can I write of course twice?

From Deb To Mark

By the way, do you know this strange, puzzle of a poem by Edward Thomas? If not, I think you might like it…

The Thrush

When Winter's ahead,
What can you read in November
That you read in April
When Winter's dead?

I hear the thrush, and I see
Him alone at the end of the lane
Near the bare poplar's tip,
Singing continuously.

Is it more that you know
Than that, even as in April,
So in November,
Winter is gone that must go?

Or is all your lore
Not to call November November,
And April April,
And Winter Winter—no more?

But I know the months all,
And their sweet names, April,
May and June and October,
As you call and call

I must remember
What died into April
And consider what will be born
Of a fair November;

And April I love for what
It was born of, and November
For what it will die in,
What they are and what they are not,

While you love what is kind,
What you can sing in
And love and forget in
All that's ahead and behind.

Edward Thomas

From Mark
To Deb

Yes, 'The Thrush' is good, complete with its nod to Hardy seeing the thrush at the end of the lane. I was thinking about how important poetry and nature and things like that are for getting perspective on business. I've just visited a series of Lush shops. In one conversation I had with staff, I realised that many of the products, treatments and fragrances that I have been responsible for creating are about prevailing and recovering – the main themes of business.

It's all to do with my mother. I visited her for her ninety-fourth birthday recently with my sister and we had fish and chips for lunch. She still has all her faculties and some money. However, she is also still overcome with fear, as she has been all her life – it's stopped her doing anything and everything. It's subtly been behind much of my aims in business. I see her, and I want everything I am involved with sorted out and all the women connected with me to fulfil their potential.

Just one more story. One of the last times Mo and I flew anywhere, we were in Manchester airport. Manchester seems to specialise in getting folk away for sunny weekends, which, as a couple who haven't flown for four years for environmental reasons, was a bit of a challenge. Anyway, that isn't the point of the story. The gate that we were flying from was forty-three minutes from the place where we were sitting down. Always a bit of a shock. We were running along, pulling our hand luggage, when about twenty-five minutes in, we reached a couple of uniformed airport staff:

'Not far now, sir,' said one. 'Nearly there, madam,' said the other.

When we've had a tough week, we say that to each other as we get into bed: 'Not far now, sir.' 'Nearly there, madam.' Although we know in truth that business is never done.

From Deb
To Mark

You're so right! Managing our success has also been difficult, although, I guess, that's a nicer problem to have! I could do with some business help that's not a bloody poem!

From Mark
To Deb

Dear Deb,

Is the Oxford Street shop doing OK? Our aim was to open a standalone Poetry Pharmacy shop in London. Do you think that the Oxford Street store is just a step along the journey?

Only poems can jolt you hard so that life takes a different angle. I'd like to place an order on the phone to the Poetry Pharmacy (to a large department store) please:

Order On The Phone To A Large Department Store

Could I order an explosion
please. As large as they come
and quite fantastic.
Would you make it out to
my account; I want it now,
to collect not posted.
It has to happen immediately,
at once, or the whole thing's
wasted. And when I see it,
for the price they charge,
I want it large, large.
With fantastic colours shooting
out of the flames, and the loudest
'bang of all bangs'.
No-one will be hurt, just shaken
and astonished. Not shocked
in the medical sense,
just jolted hard
so that life takes a different angle
and a totally new,
refreshing direction.
After all it will be a huge explosion.

Sally Heilbut

COULD I ORDER AN EXPLOSION PLEASE.

Dear Mark,

Mark, you speak of success for us looking like our own Poetry Pharmacy that's not inside Lush. While we get to grips with scaling up to cope with the demand of Oxford Street, I wanted to say that if I had any ambition, it was always an underlying mission to take poetry to people who might not otherwise encounter it, or think it was for them. In terms of my own ambitions and what success looks like, getting poetry books onto the busiest shopping street in the world is pretty good. We've made a place for poetry and this has led to other, unexpected successes like books and collaborations, and now we may have enough money to develop our business further. This is exciting, and exhausting (!) in equal measure.

I wanted to choose a poem to close this book on, and to reflect how I'm feeling about the business as we move forward. It's about moving onwards, out of the safe harbour of this mentoring relationship, not to reject it, or to not value it enormously, but maybe it's time for me to take flight...

Woman Running Alone

A woman who follows her own trail
and pounds pavements of unending cities,
past statues of forgotten men, fountains,
sticky sunshine pouring over tower blocks,
past gentrified basement windows
where wives hear the washing-up howl
between their hands, past suits on phones
and panda-eyed women in doorways
with faces that say I know, I know – tell me
about it; these streets with open hands
beg for more than is ever offered,
where someone's kid is a sleeping bag,
where the wolf-whistle becomes the wolf
and love's worn like musk aftershave,
where she forgets who she is: Ms. Keep On,
Ms. Never-going-home, neither running away
nor running toward anyone, wind-sifted,
letting the weather sing through her,
she who is different to her brothers.

The rhythm fills her with flight –
              and her wings,
                          what wings she has –

Maria Taylor

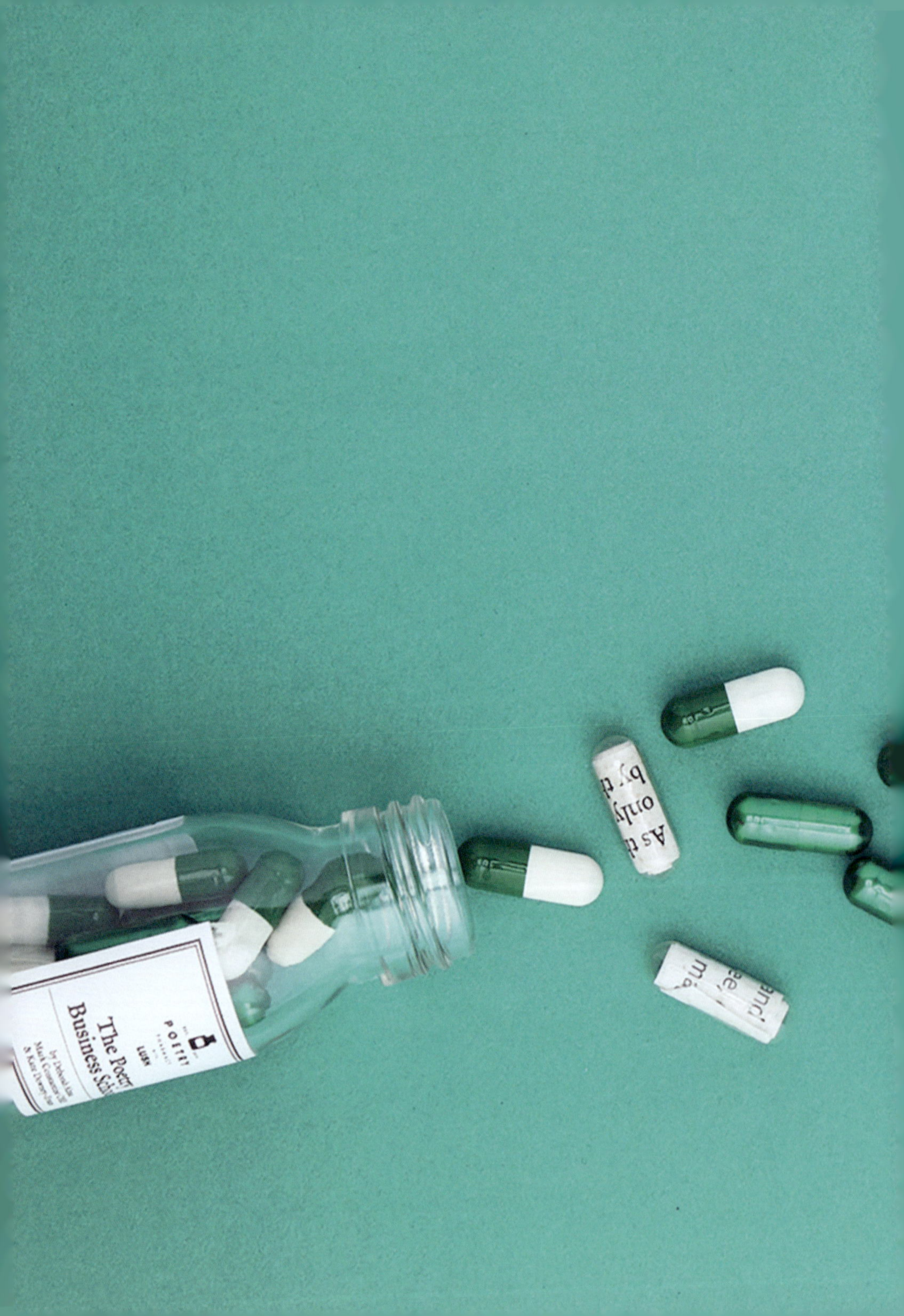

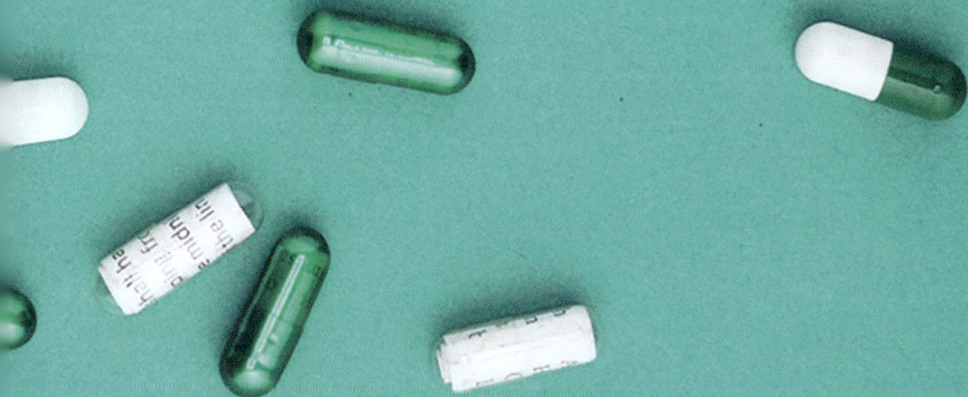

ACKNOWLEDGEMENTS

Firstly, a huge thank you to Gina Wheatley and Matt Fairhall at Lush who worked with me to stitch this book together; Matt for the painstaking work of proofreading, patience and encouragement, and thanks to Gina for staying with it with the patience of a saint and for her wisdom and kindness.

I'm so grateful to Kate Downey-Evans for her bursts of real business insight and for her contributions to the book and to me personally as a manager of my small business.

Thanks to Kayley Thomas for putting up with a poet in those early conversations, and for being so open-minded about reading poetry.

Thank you to Kate Jenkinson for speaking to me about how she uses poetry in the world of business as a Business Poet and for her poem for the book.

I'm grateful to Holly Tucker MBE for her generous foreword; Holly is a champion of the small business community and has been very kind in her support for the Poetry Pharmacy over the last few years and it was her excellent Independent Business Awards shortlist that led, in a circuitous route, to this book.

Thanks always to my partner, James Sheard, who although slightly bewildered by the idea of the book, has been so supportive, especially with cups of coffee!

And finally, to Mark himself, who has believed that the Poetry Pharmacy was a good business idea from the start and who, despite my often not listening to him, didn't give up telling me that it was a good idea. For his generosity in this and for his humour as well as the gentle nagging, I am very very grateful.
Deborah Alma

Thank you to Dr Suzanne Fairless-Aitken for all the help with permissions, and to Milly Allen and Nicky Dear for their legal support. Thank you to Suzie Hackney for setting the book's art direction, to Lily Thomas for leading on the book's artworking, to Julia Lawrence for extra artwork support and to Kate Ellistone for illustrating the front and back covers.

With special thanks to Caitlin Doyle and Mary Thompson of HarperCollins.

ILLUSTRATION AND PHOTOGRAPHY CREDITS

Illustrations

Front and back covers: © Cosmetics Warriors Limited 2024 by Kate Ellistone

Page 20: © LUSH Limited 2024 by Lily Thomas. Used with the permission of LUSH Limited

Page 23: © Cosmetic Warriors Limited 2024 by Shannon Lund

Page 27: © Sofia Iva

Page 29: © Cosmetics Warriors Limited 2024 by Suzie Hackney

Page 34: © Cosmetic Warriors Limited 2024 by Suzie Hackney

Page 38: Rohan Eason / IllustrationX

Page 40: © Cosmetic Warriors Limited 2024 by Suzie Hackney

Page 43: Gina Rosas Moncada / IllustrationX

Page 45: © Joanna Blémont

Page 47: Seatton Asamoah Daniels, © Artbox London, a supported studio for people with learning disabilities and autistic artists

Page 50: © Jeremy Sancha / Central Illustration Agency Limited

Page 55: Michael Frith / IllustrationX

Page 57: © Cosmetic Warriors Limited 2024 by Suzie Hackney

Page 59: Jeff the Peff / The Jacky Winter Group Limited

Page 60: Amy Sherratt, © ARTHOUSE Unlimited

Page 67: © Cosmetic Warriors Limited 2024 by Shannon Lund

Pages 68–69: Grace Lee / The Jacky Winter Group Limited

Page 76: © Cosmetic Warriors Limited 2024 by Kate Ellistone

Page 78: © Cosmetic Warriors Limited 2024 by Kate Ellistone

Page 80: Heedayah Lockman / IllustrationX

Page 83: Rebecca ter Borg / The Jacky Winter Group Limited

Page 85: © Cosmetic Warriors Limited 2024 by Suzie Hackney

Page 91: © Dror Cohen

Pages 96–97: Katie Edwards. © Katie Edwards

Page 103: Diego Patino / The Jacky Winter Group Limited

Page 105: © Harriet Russell / Central Illustration Agency Limited

Page 110: Sebastian Cestaro / The Jacky Winter Group Limited

Page 114: August Lamm / IllustrationX

Page 117: © Laina Deene

Page 123: Georgie Stewart / IllustrationX

Page 125: Jacquie Boyd. © Jacquie Boyd

Page 127: Nanette Hoogslag. © Nanette Hoogslag

Photography

Art Direction by Suzie Hackney
Artworking by Lily Thomas and Julia Lawrence

POEM ACKNOWLEDGEMENTS

The poems in this anthology are reprinted from the following books, all by permission of the publishers listed unless stated otherwise. Every effort has been made to trace the copyright holders of the poems published in this book. In the event that the proprietors and publishers are notified of any mistakes or omissions after publication, the editor and publishers will endeavour to rectify the position accordingly for any subsequent printing.

Thanks are due to all the copyright holders cited below for their kind permission:

Pam Ayers, *The Works* (BBC Books, 1992) © Pam Ayres, 1992, 2008. Reproduced by permission of Sheil Land Associates Ltd.

Wendell Berry, *New Collected Poems* (Counterpoint Press, 2012). Copyright © 2012 by Wendell Berry. Reprinted with the permission of The Permissions Company, LLC on behalf of Counterpoint Press, www.counterpointpress.com

John Betjeman, *John Betjeman: Collected Poems* (John Murray, 2006)

Edip Cansever, *Dirty August,* tr. Julia & Richard Tillinghast (Talisman House, USA, 2009) by kind permission of the translators Richard Tillinghast and Julia Clare Tillinghast

Wendy Cope, *Making Cocoa with Kingsley Amis* (Faber & Faber, 1986) © Wendy Cope, 1986 printed by permission of the publisher & United Agents on behalf of Wendy Cope. www.unitedagents.co.uk

Julia Darling, *Sudden Collapses in Public Places* (Arc Publications, 2003)

Seamus Heaney, *The Spirit Level* (Faber & Faber, FSG Books, 2001)

Sally Heilbut, 'Order On The Phone To A Large Department Store', permission kindly granted by the estate of Sally Heilbut

Jane Hirshfield, *The Asking: New & Selected Poems* (Bloodaxe Books, 2024) www.bloodaxebooks.com

Miroslav Holub, *Poems Before & After: Collected English Translations,* trans. Ian and Jarmila Milner et al. (Bloodaxe Books, 2006) www.bloodaxebooks.com

Kate Jenkinson, https://nextstephr.co.uk/using-the-power-of-words/ by kind permission of the author

INDEX OF POEMS, POETS AND FIRST LINES

'All The Pretty Horses' by Anon   17
Hush-by, Don't you cry

'A Pict Song' by Rudyard Kipling   23
Rome never looks where she treads.

'Naming of Parts' by Henry Reed   27
To-day we have naming of parts. Yesterday,

'Arrival' by R.S. Thomas   29
Not conscious

'What If this Road' by Sheenagh Pugh   35
What if this road, that has held no surprises

'The Road Not Taken' by Robert Frost   38
Two roads diverged in a yellow wood

'Table' by Edip Cansever   40
A man filled with the gladness of living

'An Optimistic Paean to False Starts' by Rabindranath Tagore   42
Life's honouring deeds we start and do not do –

'Evening' by Rainer Maria Rilke (translated from the German   43
by James Sheard)
The evening slowly disrobes, and hands

'Bath' by Amy Lowell   45
The day is fresh-washed and fair, and there is a smell of tulips
and narcissus in the air.

'On Reason and Passion' extract from 'The Prophet' by Kahlil Gibran 47
Your reason and your passion are the rudder and

'To A Dancing Star' by Sara Teasdale   49
Come, star, and dance with me

'Stopping by Woods on a Snowy Evening' by Robert Frost   50
Whose woods these are I think I know.

'Let Them Eat Chaos' (extract) by Kae Tempest   52
Smart flats. Rough flats.

'Under Milkwood' (extract) by Dylan Thomas   53
Morning, Mrs Ogmore-Pritchard.

'The Peace Of Wild Things' by Wendell Berry   55
When despair for the world grows in me

'The Shepherd's Calendar' (extract) by John Clare   57
The sun peeps thro the window pane

'First Fig' by Edna St. Vincent Millay   59
My candle burns at both ends;

'Postscript' by Seamus Heaney   60
And some time make the time to drive out west

'New Eyes Each Year' by Philip Larkin   64
New eyes each year

'On Giving' extract from 'The Prophet' by Kahlil Gibran   67
Then said a rich man, Speak to us of Giving.

'On Buying and Selling' extract from 'The Prophet' by Kahlil Gibran   69
When in the market-place you toilers of the sea and fields and vineyards

'Oh, I Wish I'd Looked After Me Teeth' (extract) by Pam Ayres   72
If I'd known I was paving the way

'If' by Rudyard Kipling   76
If you can keep your head when all about you

'If through finding your voice' by Kate Jenkinson   78
If through finding your voice

'Talking Turkeys!!!' (extract) by Benjamin Zephaniah   80
I once knew a turkey called... Turkey

'I Need Not Go' by Thomas Hardy   83
I need not go

'Ask Me' by William Stafford   85
Some time when the river is ice ask me

'Engineers' Corner' by Wendy Cope   89
Why isn't there an Engineers' Corner in Westminster Abbey?

'You Reading This, Be Ready' by William Stafford   91
Starting here, what do you want to remember?

'London, 1802' by William Wordsworth   93
London hath need of thee: she is a fen

'The Going' by Thomas Hardy   96-97
Why did you give no hint that night

'Poem' by Kate Downey-Evans & ChatGPT 103
In the lab where dreams take flight,

'Too Heavy' by Julia Darling 105
Dear Doctor,

'On this wondrous sea' by Emily Dickinson 109
On this wondrous sea

'The door' by Miroslav Holub (translated from the Czech by Ian Milner) 110
Go and open the door.

'Faint Heart Never Won Fair Lady' (extract) by Sir John Bowring 111
He who is both brave and bold

'I Wandered Lonely as a Cloud' by William Wordsworth 112
(Wordsworth in Covent Garden!)
I wandered lonely as a cloud

'The Weighing' by Jane Hirshfield 114
The heart's reasons

'Poem Without Ends' (extract) by Alastair Reid 119
One cannot take the beginning out of the air

'The Thrush' by Edward Thomas 123
When Winter's ahead,

'Order On The Phone To A Large Department Store' by Sally Heilbut 125
Could I order an explosion

'Woman Running Alone' by Maria Taylor 127
A woman who follows her own trail

QUOTED MATERIAL ACKNOWLEDGEMENTS

'Get me poets as managers. Poets are our original systems   5
thinkers. They look at our most complex environments
and they reduce the complexity to something they begin
to understand.'
Sidney Harman
Founder of Harman Industries

'... poetry has defined business mainly by excluding it. Business   5
does not exist in the world of poetry, and therefore by implication
it has become everything that poetry is not – a world without
imagination, enlightenment, or perception.'
Extract from *Business and Poetry* by Dana Gioia, taken from
Can Poetry Matter? Essays on Poetry and American Culture, 1983

'The world is too much with us.'   16
William Wordsworth, from 'The World Is Too Much With Us'

'to get by heart and read aloud.'   26
Clive James, from *The Fire of Joy: Roughly Eighty Poems
to Get by Heart and Read Aloud*

'In its early stages, insomnia is almost an oasis in which those who 31
have to think or suffer darkly take refuge.'
Sidonie-Gabrielle Colette

'I mean Negative Capability, that is when man is capable of being in 33
uncertainties, mysteries, doubts, without any irritable reaching after
fact and reason.'
John Keats, from a letter to his brothers George and Thomas,
21 December, 1817

'handsome, reckless, mettlesome as a stallion breathing the first   34
morning air, he would laugh at himself, indeed laugh at everything,
with a laugh that scattered melancholy as the wind scatters the
petals of the fading poppy... He had the gift of the aristocrat and
could adapt himself to all circumstances... his blood was testy,
adventurous, quixotic, and he faced life as an eagle faces its flight.'
Alyse Powers describing their friend, Eugen Boissevain

'It is not the critic who counts; not the man who points out how the 36
strong man stumbles, or where the doer of deeds could have done
them better. The credit belongs to the man who is actually in the
arena, whose face is marred by dust and sweat and blood; who
strives valiantly; who errs, who comes short again and again,

because there is no effort without error and shortcoming; but who does actually strive to do the deeds; who knows great enthusiasms, the great devotions; who spends himself in a worthy cause; who at the best knows in the end the triumph of high achievement, and who at the worst, if he fails, at least fails while daring greatly, so that his place shall never be with those cold and timid souls who neither know victory nor defeat.'
Theodore Roosevelt, former President of the United States, from his speech Citizenship in a Republic, given at the Sorbonne in Paris, France, on 23 April, 1910

'Lower: Fear of Money. Lack of financial support.' Louise Hay, from *You Can Heal Your Life*	66
'I trust the process of life. All I need is always taken care of. I am safe.' Louise Hay, from *You Can Heal Your Life*	66
'To business that we love we rise betime, And go to 't with delight.' William Shakespeare, from *Antony and Cleopatra*	75
'Never interrupt your enemy when he is making a mistake.' Napoleon Bonaparte	100
A ship in harbour is safe, but that is not what ships are built for.' John Augustus Shedd	109
'Everything is negotiable. Whether or not the negotiation is easy is another thing.' Carrie Fisher	111
'In people's eyes, in the swing, tramp, and trudge; in the bellow and the uproar; the carriages, motorcars, omnibuses, vans, sandwich men shuffling and swinging; brass bands; barrel organs; in the triumph and the jingle and the strange high singing of some aeroplane overhead was what she loved; life; London; this moment of June.' Virginia Woolf, from *Mrs Dalloway*	117

AUTHOR BIOGRAPHIES

Deborah Alma

Deborah Alma is a UK poet, editor and bookseller. She has worked using poetry with people with dementia, in hospice care, with women's groups and with children in schools, and taught at both Worcester and Keele Universities. From 2012, she has been the Emergency Poet, offering poetry on prescription from her vintage ambulance. She co-founded the world's first walk-in Poetry Pharmacy in Shropshire with her partner, the poet James Sheard, in 2019, which now has a second branch inside Lush Spa Oxford Street, London.

She is editor of Emergency Poet, an anti-stress poetry anthology; #Me Too, which rallies against sexual harassment; a women's poetry anthology, *Ten Poems of Happiness* from Candlestick Press and co-edited with Dr Katie Amiel *These Are the Hands – Poems from the Heart of the NHS*. She is also editor of *National Trust: Nature Poems*. Her first full collection *Dirty Laundry* is published by Nine Arches Press.

She is co-author of *The Poetry Business School* with Mark Constantine and is editor of the Poetry Pharmacy series with Macmillan, in 2025.

Mark Constantine OBE

Mark Constantine OBE is a British entrepreneur who co-founded Lush with five friends and creative confidants in 1995. Mark is a trichologist, perfumer and part of Lush's product development team creating hair, skincare and body creams along with transformative spa treatments. Mark is also Lush's CEO and the driving force behind the business.

In the 2010 Queen's New Years Honours list, Mark and his wife Mo Constantine both received OBEs for their services to the beauty industry. Mark has been named five times since 2010 as one of London's 1000 Most Influential People in the 'Environment' and 'Business Brains' categories by *The Evening Standard* newspaper.

Today, Lush operates in 50 countries with over 850 shops, 38 websites shipping worldwide and a global network of native apps, broadcasting channels and digital communities in over 30 languages.

Kate Downey-Evans CPsychol

Kate is a qualified Business Psychologist, with over fifteen years of experience in some of the world's largest corporations, including Bupa and HSBC. In 2019, Kate launched The Green Door Project to help both individuals and organisations discover their hidden diamonds, unlock their potential and achieve the extraordinary.

With her in-depth understanding of the science of human psychology and experience in business, Kate helps her clients to see what they are capable of, to find the freedom and fulfilment that they have been searching for.

Contributing to both personal and business growth, Kate has an impressive portfolio of work within large, multinational organisations, as well as in indigenous communities, in countries such as India, Mexico, Argentina and Indonesia. From her experiences, Kate is a firm believer in that everyone has potential to do incredible things, you just have to open the door and look inside.

Next page: Deb in the Poetry Pharmacy's new London home,
Lush Spa Oxford St, 31 May 2024.

COMFORT INSPIRATION WILD REM

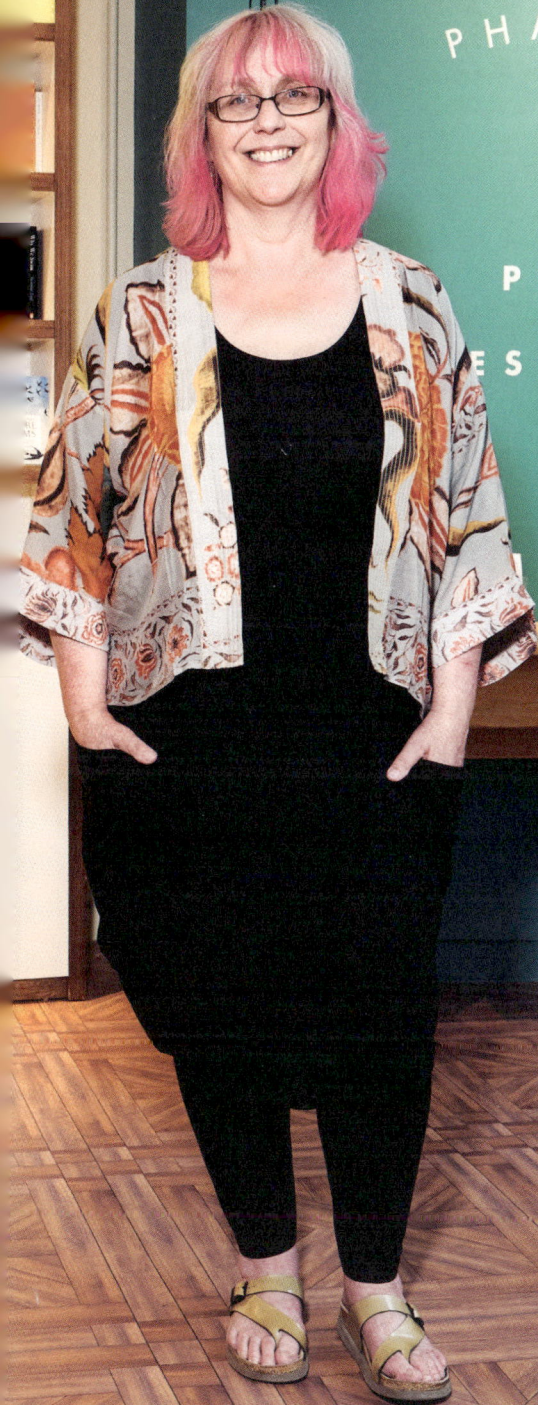

POETRY

PHARMACY

WITH

LUSH

EST. 2019